DEER-RESISTANT
NATIVE PLANTS
=== FOR THE ===
Northeast

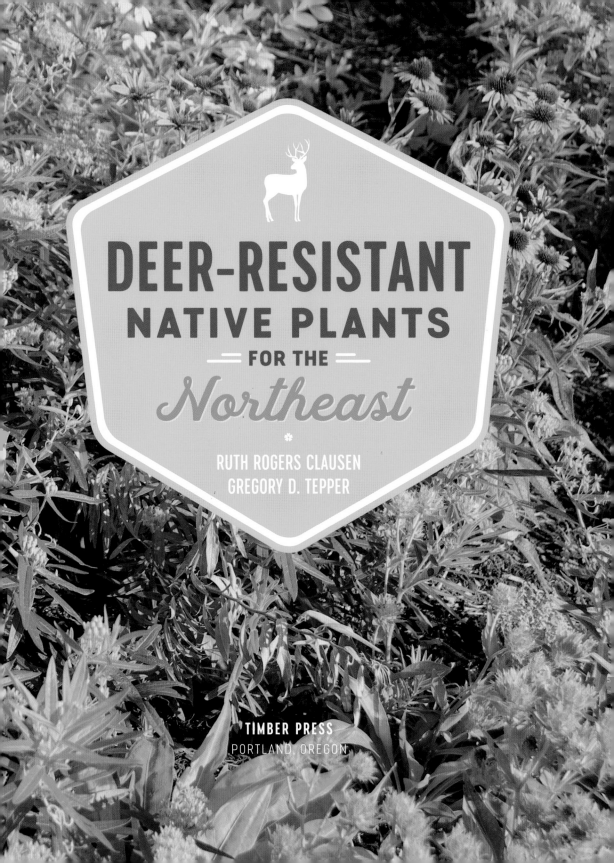

DEER-RESISTANT
NATIVE PLANTS
FOR THE
Northeast

❀

RUTH ROGERS CLAUSEN
GREGORY D. TEPPER

TIMBER PRESS
PORTLAND, OREGON

Frontispiece: Not only do the native plants featured in this book offer resistance to deer, they are truly garden-worthy and fulfill important ecological roles.
Pages 6-7: (clockwise from top left)
Rudbeckia triloba, Eutrochium maculatum, Carex platyphylla, Itea virginica, Adiantum pedatum, and *Muhlenbergia capillaris*

Published in 2021 by Timber Press, Inc.
The Haseltine Building
133 S.W. Second Avenue, Suite 450
Portland, Oregon 97204-3527
timberpress.com

Printed in China
Text and cover design by Sarah Crumb

ISBN 978-1-60469-986-9
A catalog record for this book is available from the Library of Congress.

We dedicate this book to garden lovers everywhere
who must deal with an overabundance of deer.

Contents

Acknowledgments

Because of our passion for native plants and the overabundance of deer in gardens, we felt this volume would be useful to fellow enthusiasts, both beginner and seasoned professional alike. We thank Tom Fischer at Timber Press for agreeing with us and supporting the project. We greatly appreciate the editorial help from Andrew Keys Pepper and the staff at Timber Press. Lastly, we are sincerely grateful to our various colleagues for their willingness to provide photographs that we could not supply.

From Ruth Rogers Clausen: I am grateful to Tom Christopher, Margaret Barrett, Emily Crandall, and my many garden friends for their enthusiasm and encouragement. In addition, I'd like to thank my family for their unfailing support.

From Gregory D. Tepper: I wish to express my heartfelt thanks to my dear friends and loved ones who have supported me from my beginnings in gardening with words of encouragement and love. I am most grateful, too, for having learned from those people that, though they are no longer with us, inspired me then and now. Last, much love and admiration to my co-author Ruth Rogers Clausen, who made my dream of authoring a book a reality.

Black-eyed Susans mix well with butterfly flower in the summer garden.

Introduction

The recent wave of interest in growing native plants to provide food and habitat for wildlife, from foraging birds to pollinating insects, is exciting. It has created an industry demand for attractive, gardenworthy plants that aren't just aesthetically pleasing to us, they support critical ecology in turn. Plants that were once considered simple roadside wildflowers are now sought after as attractive and enviable additions to the garden plant palette. When we garden with native plants, we provide beauty for ourselves, we take pride in feeling a sense of place, and we also benefit wildlife, most importantly our pollinators. Again, this is very exciting.

Yet with all due consideration for pollinators and wildlife, there is one animal we must also consider differently as we garden in much of North America. That is the white-tailed deer (*Odocoileus virginianus*).

White-tailed deer are always looking for an easy meal.

Deer are considered by many to be the number one obstacle for successful gardens. How many times have you heard, or experienced, "I can't grow a nice garden because the deer seem to eat EVERYTHING!"?

Deer impact the garden in several ways. One is by consuming plants, also known as herbivory, or browsing. The second is when bucks (male deer) scrape young trees and shrubs to mark territory during mating season—this is known as buck rub, or rubbing. Third, deer sometimes knock down plant material to create a rounded resting or sleeping area, known as a bed, to which they retreat daily.

Herbivory is probably the most widely experienced deer issue by gardeners, and this book aims to help gardeners make the best-informed decisions in choosing plants with that in mind.

Deer are a highly adaptable, herbivorous species that thrive in a variety of habitats, including suburban developments and backyards. They have the ability to digest a variety of plant foods, from fruits, nuts, and leaves, to grass, branches, soft bark, mushrooms, corn, alfalfa, and grass—oh my! Deer are grazers that possess keen senses of smell and hearing, and will happily search out and devour so many of the plants that seem to be popular in gardens.

(left) Deer browse damage on arborvitae. (right) Bucks wreak havoc on small trees and shrubs in late fall and winter by rubbing their antlers on them to mark their territory.

There is, of course, an order of preference, so in order to effectively deal with deer, you must learn which plants deer prefer not to eat.

Let us be clear here and now: there are very few plants that are fully deer-proof, because deer's preferences change as food supplies change. Interestingly, even if a plant contains compounds poisonous to deer, has a distasteful texture, or has highly aromatic foliage, there's no guarantee that plant won't become a deer food source if the animals are severely stressed. In the middle of summer and food is plentiful, deer will eat what smells and tastes most appealing. In winter, when food is most scarce,

Common Features of Deer-Resistant Plants

Although there is no guarantee when it comes to deer browsing, plants are much less likely to be nibbled if they have any of the following:

- Fuzzy leaves
- Tough, leathery, fibrous leaves
- Aromatic leaves
- Aromatic flowers
- Spines or bristles
- Poisonous compounds.

their need to feed far outweighs food supply, and hunger drastically outweighs preferences. That's why in winter you'll find deer eating evergreen trees and shrubs, chewing off soft bark, and nipping dormant leaf and flower buds on deciduous shrubs they don't usually bother in warmer seasons, when other options are plentiful.

The denser the population of deer, the more "deer pressure" there is on the local environment and food sources available. Deer populations have increased dramatically in the past 30 years or so, mainly due to the loss of habitat from development. Fewer wild spaces mean deer move elsewhere, and as long as there is a food source, no predators, enough cover, and no activity that controls their numbers, they increase.

To effectively deal with deer, make a strategic plan. Options in this plan could entail the use of deer repellents, and physically excluding deer from the garden with a fence, as well as planting deer-resistant plants. A deer fence, for many, is a major investment, and one that requires maintenance. Repellents and strategic planting are often much more feasible.

The market for deer repellents has many offerings, some more effective than others, and each product has its pros and cons. Several are created from the urine of other animals. These are said to be marginally effective initially; unfortunately, their efficacy is short, as the scent fades over a two-week period. These must also be reapplied after every rain event, and their smell during application is just plain unpleasant.

Other products, both liquid concentrates and granular repellents, work by either taste or odor, and contain ingredients like garlic, cayenne pepper, emulsified eggs, herbal oils, and spices like clove. Each has different guidelines for efficacy, as well as reapplication frequency. Some actually smell nice when they're applied; others are just the opposite. Some can be applied directly to all plant parts, while the instructions for others say not to apply to flowering parts. With most, the product only smells when it is freshly applied; once it dries, the scent is generally undetectable by humans. Deer, however, with their powerful sense of smell, often sense it for two to three weeks, especially when the repellent has an ingredient that acts as a spreader or sticker. One product we found highly effective has emulsified eggs, rosemary oil, and mint oil. It smells pleasant when it's applied, it dries quickly, and the eggs help it to stay put on foliage for up to thirty days, regardless of rainfall.

Electronic devices represent another market in deer deterrents. One type is motion-activated, and emits a high-frequency sound deer find uncomfortable when they approach. Another lures deer with an attractant scent, and surprises them with a small electric charge to the nose when they get close enough. Others scare deer mechanically—an example is a motion-activated device that hooks up to a garden hose, and startles them with a quick, strong burst of water. This gadget requires a constant water supply, and is only effective over a limited range, but it's reported to work well. Deer are creatures

Rudbeckia 'American Gold Rush' and *Heliopsis helianthoides* 'Bleeding Hearts' mix perfectly in the deer-resistant garden.

of habit, and once they learn these devices are nearby, they effectively stay away.

With that said, it is up to you to research each repellent option and its effectiveness based upon your garden's unique situation, but further reading on these options is readily available in gardening books, magazines, and online.

Combined with deer-resistant plants, these repellents can be effective at keeping deer browsing to a minimum. It's true that there are plenty of native plants deer do enjoy eating, but the selection that isn't high on their gourmet list is extensive!

This book focuses on seventy-five native plants that deer seldom browse, categorized by type: annuals and biennials; perennials; ferns; grasses; sedges; and shrubs. A brief introduction begins each plant type chapter. This is followed by plant entries, each arranged in alphabetical order by botanical name, followed by common name. It is prudent to remember that common names are not reliable for identification and purchasing purposes, as they often differ in different parts of the country—moreover, most plants have multiple common names. Botanical names, on the other hand,

[above] Northern maidenhair fern and wild ginger work beautifully together in this shady nook. [right] A fall medley of native, deer-resistant shrubs and perennials.

Additional Tips for Discouraging Deer

1. Fido may be helpful! When dogs are present on a site and within a garden, their scent is left behind, and deer often avoid the area.

2. Plant drought-tolerant or xeric plants with spines or fibrous stems. Many drought-tolerant plants also have tough or fuzzy foliage deer do not like.

3. Avoid overwatering and fertilizer. The soft, lush growth of plants that have been over-watered and over-fertilized is more appealing to deer than the foliage of plants that have not.

4. Water with drip or soaker hoses close to the ground to avoid wetting leaves. Deer are thirsty too, and drawn to plants with wet foliage.

5. Do not allow acorns, crabapples, or other tempting fruits to remain on the ground. These food sources will attract deer to your garden even if it is deer resistant.

6. Where possible, prune trees and large shrubs that may be browsed up to about 4 ft. high—deer cannot reach above 4 ft.

7. Elevate bird feeders beyond the reach of deer.

8. Raise plants in hanging baskets out of reach, and spray ground-level containers with repellent.

9. Plant deer-resistant native plants!

10. Avoid known deer favorites (also known as deer candy; see next page), which include a few natives.

Deer Resistance Ratings

Each plant's deer resistance is rated on a scale from 7 to 10. Note that plants rated lower than 7, those regularly browsed by deer, are not included in this book.

7 – Deer sometimes nip off flowers, but leave foliage alone

8 – Deer occasionally nip off one or two flowers, but mostly ignore the plant

9 – Deer occasionally browse young spring foliage, but mostly ignore the plant

10 – Deer rarely browse foliage or flowers, and usually avoid plant altogether

remain consistent worldwide, for the most part. To select a particular species from a plant catalog or list, it is critical to be able to refer to it by its botanical name.

Each plant entry begins with its botanical and common names, plant family, and a box with its deer-resistance rating (see left); hardiness zones (find yours at planthardiness. ars.usda.gov); states in the Northeast where the plant is native, mostly referenced from the Lady Bird Wildflower Center website (www. wildflower.org); and size in height and spread. Following that is a descriptive narrative, and where applicable, a discussion of cultivated varieties (or cultivars for short) and additional deer-resistant species within that genus—these bonus plants greatly increase the number at your disposal. Each plant's narrative is followed by information on culture and tips, suggested companion plants discussed elsewhere in the text, and a short paragraph entitled "Did you know?" that provides unique facts and a roundup of wildlife that particular plant attracts.

Based on the authors' experiences, the plants included here all do well in northeastern and mid-Atlantic gardens, although these regions don't necessarily encompass their native ranges in the strict sense.

Deer Candy: Native Plants Deer Prefer!

These are just a few of the native plants that will *attract* deer to your garden. Either avoid planting them, or plan to protect them with physical barriers or routine repellent spraying.

- Eastern redbud (*Cercis canadensis*)
- Lady's slipper (*Cypripedium* species)
- Wild geranium (*Geranium maculatum*)
- Alumroot (*Heuchera* species)
- Smooth hydrangea (*Hydrangea arborescens*)
- Juniper (*Juniperus virginiana*)
- Lily (*Lilium* species)
- Canada mayflower (*Maianthemum canadense*)
- Native crabapple (*Malus coronaria*)
- Native phlox (*Phlox* species)
- Native deciduous azalea (*Rhododendron* species)
- Elderberry (*Sambucus canadensis*)
- Snowberry (*Symphoricarpos albus*)
- Eastern arborvitae (*Thuja occidentalis*)
- Trillium (*Trillium* species)

Annuals AND Biennials

Annuals are plants that complete their life cycle in a single growing season; that is, their seeds are sown; germinate; grow stems, leaves, and flowers; and produce seeds for following generations in that timespan. Annuals include many familiar summer flowers, such as nasturtiums and zinnias, as well as herbs like sweet basil and dill. Certain weeds, like chickweed and crabgrass, are also annuals. Annuals can be delightful to use in the garden, as they grow fast and often bloom profusely. Besides that, the gardener can reposition annuals from year to year simply based on where they decide to sow seeds.

Biennials are unique plants that complete their life cycle within two growing seasons. Once their seeds are sown, they germinate and grow on quickly, yet they don't flower that first season. These plants overwinter successfully in a vegetative state, and the following spring, they grow much larger and begin flowering early on. Once flowering is finished, in late spring into summer, their seedpods mature, shed their seed, and the plant dies. The seeds that were dropped germinate later that season, and the entire growth process starts again. Hollyhock and foxglove are well-known biennials grown for their flowers, and well-known biennial vegetables include cabbage and Brussels sprouts. Like annuals, biennials offer quick growth and abundant flowering, and make an ever-changing show in the garden.

We have selected ten native annuals and biennials that, in our experience, are reliably deer resistant.

Bidens aristosa DAISY FAMILY (ASTERACEAE)

Bearded beggar-ticks, swamp marigold

DEER RESISTANCE	HARDINESS ZONES	NORTHEAST NATIVE STATES	HEIGHT/SPREAD
8-10	6-11	CT, DC, DE, MA, MD, ME, NH, NJ, NY, PA, VA, WV	12-60 IN. × 12-36 IN.

In summer, yellow, daisy-shaped flowers abound in the wild, and there are a few worth bringing into the garden. Upright, bearded beggar-ticks makes a bold annual statement in the later summer garden with its 1-2 in. wide brilliant golden flower heads. Several solitary heads are carried on wiry, multi-branching stems. Alternate, divided leaves are composed of several opposite leaflets, each with a smaller terminal one. Leaflets are toothed along the edges, and hairy beneath.

Species of bearded beggar-ticks have become more widely grown due to recent efforts in breeding. Of note are dwarf *B. aristosa* Doubloon (4-6 in. × 8-12 in.) and *B. ferulifolia* Goldilocks Rocks (8-14 in. × 10-20 in.).

CULTURE AND TIPS

Bearded beggar-ticks thrives in full sun where soil is moist and even wet, but also does well in dryer locations such as prairies. This plant does not do well in shade. In the wild, it often occurs by the thousands in its preferred moist, rich soil, and is at its best when massed. Under these conditions, it can reseed aggressively. Lovely in containers, cottage gardens, damp native plant gardens as well as more formal beds and borders. Its seed should be started from late summer to fall for spring germination.

Bidens aristosa blooms profusely in late summer.

COMPANION PLANTS

In full sun, match bearded beggar-ticks with other deer-resistant natives like annual partridge pea (*Chamaecrista fasciculata*) and perennial blue mistflower (*Conoclinium coelestinum*). Shrubby Carolina allspice (*Calycanthus floridus*) also makes a fine companion, along with summersweet (*Clethra alnifolia*) over a long period, especially in fall, when the shrub's foliage turns from green to bright yellow.

DID YOU KNOW?

The seeds of bearded beggar-ticks are enclosed in a two-barbed, tick-shaped, dry fruit known as an achene. Paired barbs attach themselves to the fur of passing mammals—and perhaps your clothing—so they may be deposited some distance from the mother plant. The seeds provide food for birds, including northern bobwhite and other quail. In late summer and fall, late-blooming flower heads attract bees and butterflies foraging for pollen and nectar. Honeybees feeding on this plant produce dark, excellently flavored honey.

23

Capnoides sempervirens FUMITORY FAMILY (FUMARIACEAE)

Harlequin corydalis, rock harlequin

DEER RESISTANCE	HARDINESS ZONES	NORTHEAST NATIVE STATES	HEIGHT/SPREAD
9–10	5–9	CT, MA, MD, ME, NH, NJ, NY, PA, RI, VA, VT, WV	12–30 IN. × 12–20 IN.

Rosy to deep pink, tubular, ½-in. flowers, yellow and spreading at the mouth, droop in clumps of wiry stems in sprays, also called racemes. Each bloom is composed of two pairs of petals, with a short, rounded spur at the top. Erect stems carry fernlike, bluish gray-green compound

The flowers of harlequin corydalis are a lovely pink and yellow bicolor.

leaves, further divided into rounded segments. Bloom continues sporadically from late spring to early fall, producing slender seedpods throughout the season. Left undisturbed, the seedpods will shed seeds to bloom the following year.

Because it can seed about, this plant is perfect in rock gardens, on the edge of gravel pathways, and for fissures in rock walls. An annual or biennial, harlequin corydalis features an open, airy habit that is most suitable for small, unique sections of garden space where other plants may not grow. It is also known as *Corydalis sempervirens*.

CULTURE AND TIPS

Best in full or part sun, harlequin corydalis is not fussy about soil as long as it drains well. In the wild, it thrives in poor, rocky, acid soil. It grows readily from seed, will reseed if allowed, and will overwinter as rosettes of vegetative growth

Capnoides sempervirens, an easy-to-grow biennial, blooms for months on end.

for bloom the following year. Plants can be started successfully indoors, and young plants can be transplanted where desired to enable taproot development. To accomplish seeding into crevices or rock walls, cut a 1-in. piece off the end of a drinking straw, horizontally, to make a shelf. Then place seeds on this shelf, and blow gently into soil-filled niches between the stones. Firm and spray with water to maintain moisture until germination occurs.

COMPANION PLANTS

Harlequin corydalis is best partnered with other woodland plants, such as annual blue-eyed Mary (*Collinsia verna*); biennial purple phacelia (*Phacelia bipinnatifida*); or perennials like red columbine (*Aquilegia canadensis*), green-and-gold (*Chrysogonum virginianum*), rue-anemone (*Thalictrum thalictroides*), wild bleeding heart (*Dicentra eximia*), and ostrich fern (*Matteuccia struthiopteris*).

DID YOU KNOW?

The seeds of harlequin corydalis bear white fleshy structures called elaiosomes on their surface. Full of fats and proteins, they're a food source for foraging ants, which carry the seed back to their nests underground. Ants discard the seeds after feeding, and this process ensures the seeds' distribution. In the wild, harlequin corydalis is often found in areas of disturbance.

Centaurea americana DAISY FAMILY (ASTERACEAE)

American star-thistle, basket flower

DEER RESISTANCE	HARDINESS ZONES	NORTHEAST NATIVE STATES	HEIGHT/SPREAD
7-9	2-8	NY, RI	18-60 IN. × 24-30 IN.

American star-thistle has branching stems that bear rough, lance-shaped leaves alternately along their length. Over several weeks from early to midsummer, these are topped with fragrant, 4-5 in. wide flowers reminiscent of shaving brushes. The bracts that cover the lower buds are straw-colored, much like the color of a woven basket, hence the common name. The flowers have a myriad of slender petals that are mostly lavender-pink with cream in the centers, fading to white, and make excellent cut flowers, fresh or dried. After bloom, the wicker-like bracts are still attractive, and extend the flowers' season of interest. Plant in groups for impact, especially toward the back of borders, in meadow gardens, and in native plant gardens.

CULTURE AND TIPS

Select a spot for star-thistle in full sun, where soil is fertile and drains well. A neutral to slightly alkaline soil is preferable. Start seeds outside after danger of frost has passed and soil has warmed; repeat sow in midsummer for fall bloom. Mature plants are drought resistant. Deadhead spent flowers to encourage further bloom, and to avoid excessive self-seeding. Some plants may behave as short-lived perennials in mild climates. Collect seed from spent flowers as it ripens to save for sowing next spring.

COMPANION PLANTS

Suggested companions for American star-thistle include beebalm (*Monarda didyma*), with its aromatic, minty foliage and pollinator-attracting

Centaurea americana is known commonly as American star-thistle.

flower heads; and red-flowering cultivars of yarrow (*Achillea millefolium*) like 'Fire King'. It is well complemented by the bright blooms of annual sneezeweed (*Helenium amarum*), perennial orange coneflower (*Rudbeckia fulgida*), and false sunflower (*Helianthus helianthoides*). The foliage and towering flowers of prairie rosinweed (*Silphium terebinthinaceum*) make it a fitting companion.

DID YOU KNOW?

The flower heads of American star-thistle are regularly visited by several species of bumble-bees for protein-rich pollen and nectar. Hummingbirds, songbirds, butterflies, and many insect pollinators are frequent guests. Seeds provide food for goldfinches and other seed-eating birds in fall.

Chamaecrista fasciculata PEA FAMILY (FABACEAE)

Partridge pea, sleeping pea

DEER RESISTANCE	HARDINESS ZONES	NORTHEAST NATIVE STATES	HEIGHT/SPREAD
7-8	3-9	CT, DC, DE, MA, MD, NJ, NY, PA, RI, VA,WV	12-36 IN. × 12-36 IN.

Annual, upright-growing partridge pea has delicate yellowish green, pinnately compound leaves, with eight to fifteen pairs of leaflets that often close together when disturbed. From early summer to frost, bright yellow, ½- to 1-in. flowers, each accented with a central red dot, put on their display, followed by slender maroon seedpods typical of the pea family.

This plant is helpful in native plant gardens and meadows, where it improves soil fertility with nitrogen-fixing bacteria attached to its roots. Partridge pea is most effective en masse, and makes an excellent choice for large-scale plantings because it self-sows prolifically. Given that, its use in small gardens requires careful monitoring.

CULTURE AND TIPS

Partridge pea does best in gravelly or sandy loam soils in full to part sun, and grows deep taproots that enable the plants to tolerate dry periods. Start seeds in early spring or in mid-fall. For spring sowing, nick the seed and soak overnight to ensure speedy germination. Scatter seeds where you intend them to grow, and germination should occur in one to two weeks. Thereafter the plant will self-sow freely. For mid-fall sowing, plant seed intact where it is intended to grow; it will germinate the following spring, and subsequently self-seed.

COMPANION PLANTS

Partridge pea mingles well with other annuals and biennials for sun, like bearded beggar-ticks (*Bidens aristosa*) and brown-eyed Susan (*Rudbeckia triloba*). Native grasses make great companions, especially little bluestem (*Schizachyrium scoparium*) and switchgrass (*Panicum virgatum*). Nodding onion (*Allium cernuum*), butterfly flower (*Asclepias tuberosa*), and blanket flower (*Gaillardia pulchella*) offer interesting perennial complements and contrasts. The silvery green flowers and archi-tectural habit of rattlesnake master (*Eryngium yuccifolium*) provide strong contrast.

DID YOU KNOW?

Seeds of partridge pea may be planted on the edge of banks and ditches to help control erosion. The flowers produce both pollen and nectar through glands on the leaf petioles. It is the host plant for sleepy orange, little yellow, and cloudless sulphur caterpillars. Partridge pea attracts several species of long-tongued bumblebees and leaf-cutting bees, along with sweat bees, ants, and wasps. It is sometimes grown for honey production.

Chamaecrista fasciculata makes an excellent annual addition to native meadows and other naturalized areas.

Collinsia verna FIGWORT FAMILY (SCROPHULARIACEAE)

Blue-eyed Mary, Chinese houses

DEER RESISTANCE	HARDINESS ZONES	NORTHEAST NATIVE STATES	HEIGHT/SPREAD
8-10	2-11	NY, PA, VA, WV	6-24 IN. × 8-12 IN.

In early spring, a mass of annual blue-eyed Mary is a delight to discover, its unusual ¾-in. flowers bicolored in blue and white. Each bloom has two well-defined lips, the bright white upper lip and true blue lower lip, each with two notched lobes. A very small third lip is hidden between the larger, lower ones. Carried on slender stems, the flowers may be solitary or appear five to six in a group. Blue-eyed Mary's opposite leaves are about 2 in. long, slightly pubescent, and typically have lightly toothed margins.

In late spring, with the onset of warmer temperatures, plants go to seed and die thereafter. Each flower generally produces four seeds. These drop and remain dormant until early fall, when they germinate. Those young plants persist through winter, and bloom in early spring.

CULTURE AND TIPS

In the wild, blue-eyed Mary thrives in consistently moist woodland environments with fertile, well-drained soils high in organic matter. Replicating these conditions in the garden will ensure success. When first introducing this plant to the garden by seed, direct sow where proper conditions exist, and protect young plants from drying out. Seed can be started in pots and then transplanted to the garden once plants have grown several leaves. Be mindful, however, not to disturb taproots. Because this winter annual needs to reseed to perpetuate, care should be taken to allow young plants to establish in a site that is not heavily mulched or disturbed. It is best to mark off an area where young plants are developing.

COMPANION PLANTS

Harlequin corydalis (*Capnoides sempervirens*) and purple phacelia (*Phacelia bipinnatifida*) make excellent annual companions. Perennial green-and-gold (*Chrysogonum virginianum*), red columbine (*Aquilegia canadensis*), and rue-anemone (*Thalictrum thalictroides*) interspersed

Collinsia verna is a sight to behold in early spring.

with seersucker sedge (*Carex plantaginea*) provide an interesting mixture of habits, textures, and flower combinations. Spicebush (*Lindera benzoin*) forms an ideal shrubby backdrop.

DID YOU KNOW?

Blue-eyed Mary makes a good cut flower with a long vase life. Bumblebees and other long-tongued bees visit early for pollen and nectar. Interestingly, the plant is self-pollinated, but only about half of its pollen tubes actually grow enough to fertilize its egg cells. Blue-eyed Mary is a host plant for the caterpillars of spring and summer azure butterflies. Its genus, *Collinsia*, was named for a prominent Philadelphia botanist of the early 1800s, Zaccheus Collins.

Coreopsis tinctoria DAISY FAMILY (ASTERACEAE)

Plains tickseed, dyer's tickseed

DEER RESISTANCE	HARDINESS ZONES	NORTHEAST NATIVE STATES	HEIGHT/SPREAD
9-10	2-11	CT, DC, DE, MA, MD, ME, NJ, NY, PA, RI, VA, VT, WV	12-48 IN. × 12-18 IN.

Whether a mass planting within a meadow or a small grouping within the garden, annual plains tickseed is guaranteed to be absolutely stunning. This conspicuous, easy-to-grow annual blooms over an extended period, making it a good option for color in numerous garden locations, including beds and borders, native plant gardens, and herb gardens, as well as containers. The 2-in. wide daisy-shaped blooms are also good for cutting. Flower heads have notched, bright yellow rays centered with deep red-maroon, and a purplish disc. These are carried on upright, slender, branched stems in small groups.

'Roulette' (12-24 in. × 12-18 in.) is a compact, semi-double selection with deep mahogany-rayed flowers striped with bright gold.

CULTURE AND TIPS

Start from seed indoors four to six weeks or so before the last expected frost, or outdoors after danger of frost has passed. Press the seeds gently into the soil, but do not cover, as light is necessary for germination. Plains tickseed thrives in full or part sun in average to poor soils. It does not demand much water, but tolerates poor drainage where others may not thrive. Sandy or loamy soils work well, given sufficient moisture. Deadhead spent flowers routinely to extend bloom time.

COMPANION PLANTS

Many deer-resistant natives combine beautifully with plains tickseed. Try switchgrass (*Panicum virgatum*) and prairie dropseed (*Sporobolus*

Coreopsis tinctoria is available in many color variations of red and yellow.

heterolepis) for texture. Blue false indigo (*Baptisia australis*) blooms somewhat earlier, but its blue-green foliage and strong stems support and embellish tickseed's bright daisy-like flowers. Blue flowers also provide dramatic contrast with its shade of yellow—check out azure sage (*Salvia azurea*) and its variety *grandiflora*. Other daisy-like flowers serve as an echo for tickseed, including black-eyed Susan (*Rudbeckia* species), coneflower (*Echinacea purpurea*), and rosinweed (*Silphium* species).

DID YOU KNOW?

Plants with "*tinctoria*" in their name refer to their use as dye plants, and this species of tickseed was a valuable source of red and yellow fabric dye in the past. Pollinators, including bees, butterflies, and assorted insects are attracted to the brilliant flower heads of plains tickseed. As an annual, this is an excellent starter plant for pollinator gardens, as its open habit allows for other perennials to become established with less competition.

Gaillardia pulchella DAISY FAMILY (ASTERACEAE)

Blanket flower, firewheel

DEER RESISTANCE	HARDINESS ZONES	NORTHEAST NATIVE STATES	HEIGHT/SPREAD
9-10	2-11	CT, DC, DE, MA, MD, ME, NJ, NY, PA, RI, VA, VT, WV	12-24 IN. × 6-12 IN.

Blanket flower is an excellent, easy-to-grow annual in sunny meadows and native gardens, as well as more formal sites in full sun. It is valued as a long-lasting cut flower. The bicolored, daisy-like, 2-in. flower heads are composed of brilliant rusty-red ray petals, two- or three-lobed and yellow at the tips, with a red central disc.

Annual blanket flower has been the subject of extensive breeding with perennial *Gaillardia* species. This has resulted in many new perennial color and flower combinations. Popular hybrid selections include 'Oranges and Lemons' (18-24 in. × 18-24 in.), 'Goblin' (10-12 in. × 12-15 in.), 'Arizona Apricot' (10-12 in. × 10-12 in.), and 'Dazzler' or 'Baby Cole' (6-8 in. × 10-12 in.).

CULTURE AND TIPS

This brilliantly colored annual demands full sun in average, well-drained soils, especially sandy or loamy ones. In cold winter zones, start seed of blanket flower with protection about six to eight weeks before the last expected frost. Transplant seedlings into assigned spots, about 12 in. apart, after risk of frost has passed. Where winter is milder, sow in fall while soil remains warm by scratching seed into the surface of prepared soil and tamping in gently before watering. This plant requires regular moisture at first, but once established, it tolerates heat and drought in summer. Deadheading extends blanket flower's period of bloom considerably. At the end of the season, allow the final round of spent flower heads to remain to drop seeds and ensure bloom the following year. Fortunately, neither deer nor rabbits care to eat this plant.

COMPANION PLANTS

In the wild, annual blanket flower can often be found growing with various grasses such as switchgrass (*Panicum virgatum*), little bluestem (*Schizachrium scoparium*), and prairie dropseed (*Sporobolus heterolepis*). Additional flowering

Gaillardia pulchella thrives in free-draining soils, and many cultivars are available.

plants that complement blanket flower are Maryland senna (*Senna marilandica*), prairie rosinweed (*Silphium terebinthinaceum*), and dense blazing star (*Liatris spicata*). Shrubby St. John's wort (*Hypericum prolificum*) and Carolina allspice (*Calycanthus floridus*) make excellent woody companions.

DID YOU KNOW?

The common name "blanket flower" probably refers to the similarity in flower coloration to the beautiful colored blankets made by Native Americans in the Southwest. Numerous bees are attracted to blanket flower for nectar and pollen, including bumblebees and green metallic sweat bees, while the foliage is a larval food for the red-and-yellow-painted schinia moth. The plant's long bloom time from summer to frost provides pollinators with food into fall. Its seeds are a favorite of goldfinches.

Helenium amarum DAISY FAMILY (ASTERACEAE)

Yellow sneezeweed, bitterweed

DEER RESISTANCE	HARDINESS ZONES	NORTHEAST NATIVE STATES	HEIGHT/SPREAD
9-10	3-10	CT, MA, MD, PA, VA	12–24 IN. × 9-15 IN.

Another outstanding annual in the daisy family, yellow sneezeweed bears the typical daisy-shaped flower heads featuring six to eight drooping, yellow ray petals that are wedge-shaped and three-lobed at the tips. The disc is typically yellow, but occasionally tinted with brown. Upright and aromatic, this thread-leaved plant branches low, and flower heads are borne at the tips of stems from midsummer into fall.

This diminutive species of *Helenium* is exceptional when massed along sidewalks, as bright flowerbed edging, and within containers and window boxes. 'Dakota Gold' is a dependable cultivar that blooms from late spring to early autumn.

CULTURE AND TIPS

Yellow sneezeweed thrives in full sun and well-drained dry to gravelly soils. This annual will not accept wet or heavy clay soils. Once established, it is very drought tolerant. Regular deadheading will help to extend bloom time; at the end of the season, remaining flower heads will self-seed and germinate the following year.

COMPANION PLANTS

In meadows and sunny wildflower gardens, multiple clusters of yellow sneezeweed are effective when tucked in between the clumps of pink muhly grass (*Muhlenbergia capillaris*) and prairie dropseed (*Sporobolus heterolepis*).

Helenium amarum blooms brightly midsummer through fall.

Lyre-leaf sage (*Salvia lyrata*), blanket flower (*Gaillardia pulchella*), smallhead blazing star (*Liatris microcephala*), and pink cultivars of yarrow (*Achillea millefolium*) like 'Richard Nelson' are perfect accompaniments for a matrix planting.

DID YOU KNOW?

Yellow sneezeweed produces abundant nectar and pollen that attracts numerous small bees, including sweat bees, as well as wasps and butterflies. All mammals avoid this plant because it contains a bitter glycoside compound called gudaldin.

Phacelia bipinnatifida BORAGE FAMILY (BORAGINACEAE)

Purple phacelia, fernleaf phacelia

DEER RESISTANCE	HARDINESS ZONES	NORTHEAST NATIVE STATES	HEIGHT/SPREAD
8-10	3-8	MD, PA, VA, WV	12-24 IN. × 18-24 IN.

Purple phacelia is a showy biennial underused in ornamental gardens because it can only be grown from seed. It is most attractive in the dappled shade of woodlands, or as an ephemeral groundcover among deciduous shrubs. In its second season, it produces quantities of violet, cup-shaped, 1/2- to 1-in. flowers over a long period. In early spring, new growth appears with light green ferny leaves carried on loose branches. One-sided, coiled clusters of buds at the tips (known as scorpioid cymes) open to nodding flowers in shades from lavender to dark purple, with white centers.

This ephemeral puts on its floral display from early to mid-spring, then fades and goes to seed in late spring. In favorable conditions, plants self-seed freely, and colonize large areas with stunning results.

Two additional *Phacelia* species of ornamental merit are annual lacy phacelia (*P. tanacetifolia*) and biennial Miami mist or fringed phacelia (*P. purshii*).

CULTURE AND TIPS

Purple phacelia is introduced to the garden by seed. It thrives in organic, acidic, moist soils, although it tolerates alkaline soil too. Select a spot in part to full shade, and in late spring to early summer, direct sow seed outdoors at the intended site. Germination occurs sporadically in early summer; the seedlings grow slowly and persist through fall and winter. Early the following spring, the young plants grow quickly, and by mid-spring are in full flower. To save seed from purple phacelia, harvest several almost-spent plants just before they finish flowering

Phacelia bipinnatafida graces the garden with flowers late April to early May.

at the end of the season and place them, tips down, in a paper bag. The seed will drop into the bag over the next few weeks. Harvest and sprinkle in an area you'd like to establish a colony.

COMPANION PLANTS

Plants typical of woodland sites are the most suitable companions for purple phacelia. A few good choices are Christmas fern (*Polystichum acrostichoides*), marginal wood fern (*Dryopteris marginalis*), red columbine (*Aquilegia canadensis*), Jacob's ladder (*Polemonium reptans*), and wild bleeding heart (*Dicentra eximia*). Round out the group with shrubby fetterbush (*Eubotrys racemosus*) and silver sedge (*Carex platyphylla*).

DID YOU KNOW?

Several different kinds of long- and short-tongued bees visit this plant to collect pollen and nectar on a regular basis, including honey and mason bees. Wasps, skipper butterflies, and other pollinators are also frequent visitors, especially where plants have naturalized en masse.

Rudbeckia triloba DAISY FAMILY (ASTERACEAE)

Brown-eyed Susan, thin-leaved coneflower

DEER RESISTANCE	HARDINESS ZONES	NORTHEAST NATIVE STATES	HEIGHT/SPREAD
9-10	4-8	CT, DC, DE, MA, MD, NJ, NY, PA, VA, VT	24-60 IN. × 12-18 IN.

Brown-eyed Susan (*R. triloba*) may be less familiar to gardeners than perennial species of *Rudbeckia*, like black-eyed Susan (*R. hirta*) and orange coneflower (*R. fulgida*). A low-maintenance biennial or short-lived perennial, this elegant plant puts on a tremendous floral display in late summer to early fall, with flowers smaller than those of the perennial species. Stems that bristle with small, white hairs are topped with 1½- to 2-in. wide flower heads that feature ray petals in bright gold, accented by flattened, brown-black disks. Hairy, ovate leaves, usually serrated along the edge, are three-lobed on the lower part of the plant.

Brown-eyed Susan's tolerance for pests, heat, and drought are much appreciated, especially toward the end of the season, and it is an excellent, long-lasting cut flower.

Two recommended cultivars are 'Prairie Glow', which features yellow-tipped petals of deep orange, and 'Blackjack Gold', which purportedly blooms over a longer season than the straight species.

CULTURE AND TIPS
Brown-eyed Susan is easy to grow in average, well-drained soils in full sun, though it tolerates part sun. Start seed indoors with protection, or wait until after the last frost to direct sow outdoors, thinning seedlings to 12 to 15 in. apart. Beware of slug and snail damage, especially to young seedlings. This plant seeds itself freely, and often naturalizes to form masses. To control self-seeding, remove some of the spent flowers; those that remain will be valuable to seed-eating songbirds.

COMPANION PLANTS

Native ornamental grasses like muhly grass, (*Muhlenbergia capillaris*) and switchgrass (*Panicum virgatum*) are attractive companions for brown-eyed Susan. For annuals, try partridge pea (*Chamaecrista fasciculata*) and plains tickseed (*Coreopsis tinctoria*). New York ironweed (*Vernonia novaboracensis*), cardinal flower (*Lobelia cardinalis*), Joe-Pye weed (*Eutrochium* spp.), and Maryland senna (*Senna marilandica*) are all reliable perennial companions.

DID YOU KNOW?

The genus *Rudbeckia* was named for a father and his son, both named Olaf Rudbeck, professors at Uppsala University in Sweden. The species name *triloba* describes the three-lobed shape of the lower leaves. Countless species of bees and butterflies are drawn to the flowers of brown-eyed Susan for nectar, so the plant is often included in butterfly and hummingbird gardens, especially to provide sustenance to pollinators late in the season.

Rudbeckia triloba is a stalwart of the late-season garden.

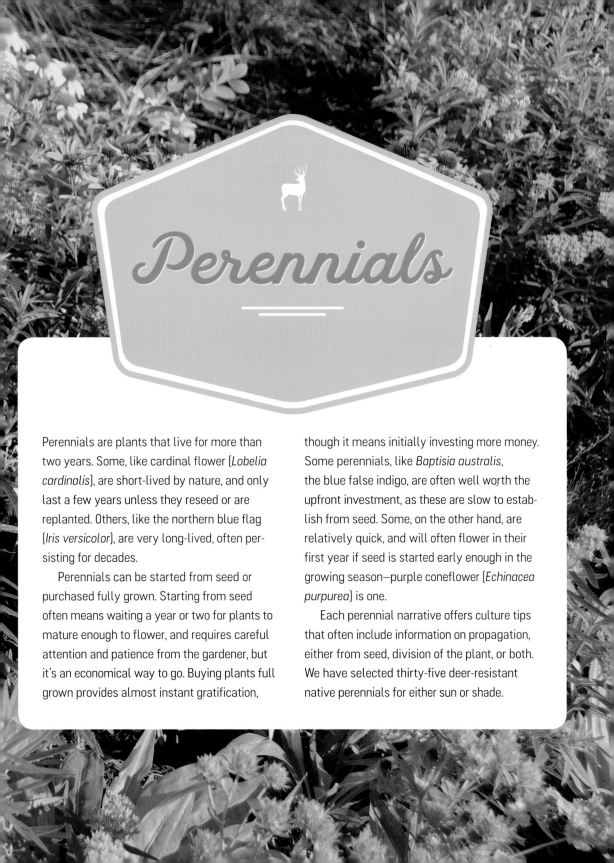

Perennials

Perennials are plants that live for more than two years. Some, like cardinal flower (*Lobelia cardinalis*), are short-lived by nature, and only last a few years unless they reseed or are replanted. Others, like the northern blue flag (*Iris versicolor*), are very long-lived, often persisting for decades.

Perennials can be started from seed or purchased fully grown. Starting from seed often means waiting a year or two for plants to mature enough to flower, and requires careful attention and patience from the gardener, but it's an economical way to go. Buying plants full grown provides almost instant gratification,

though it means initially investing more money. Some perennials, like *Baptisia australis*, the blue false indigo, are often well worth the upfront investment, as these are slow to establish from seed. Some, on the other hand, are relatively quick, and will often flower in their first year if seed is started early enough in the growing season—purple coneflower (*Echinacea purpurea*) is one.

Each perennial narrative offers culture tips that often include information on propagation, either from seed, division of the plant, or both. We have selected thirty-five deer-resistant native perennials for either sun or shade.

Achillea millefolium DAISY FAMILY (ASTERACEAE)

Common yarrow, soldier's friend

DEER RESISTANCE	HARDINESS ZONES	NORTHEAST NATIVE STATES	HEIGHT/SPREAD
8-10	3-9	CT, DC, DE, MA, MD, ME, NH, NJ, NY, PA, RI, VA, VT, WV	12-30 IN. × 24-60 IN.

Fibrous stems bear feathery silvery or green foliage, and are topped with flat heads of many tiny white flowers. Although some may consider the straight species invasive and weedy, its tough constitution has been the basis of countless superior named cultivars and varieties.

Selections of this drought-resistant plant have evolved into many color forms. Rusty orange 'Terracotta', reddish orange 'Paprika', bright red 'Fire King', pale pink 'Richard Nelson', pale lemon 'Anthea', and deep pink 'Balvinrose' are some excellent examples. It's easy to find suitable locations for yarrow in most sites, as it thrives in mixed and perennial gardens, and actually performs better in poor soils. It can be featured successfully in native plant, pollinator, and cut flower gardens, as well as rock gardens. For use in rock gardens and for containers, consider the compact Seduction Series, which grows less than 2 ft. tall: silvery-leaved rose pink 'Saucy Seduction' and buttery 'Sunny Seduction'; or green-foliaged, red-flowered 'Strawberry Seduction'. The Summer Pastel Series comes in all flower colors except blue, all paired with green foliage. Reputedly, the Song Siren Series is more tolerant of humid summer conditions.

CULTURE AND TIPS

Provide full sun and poor to average soil for yarrow to show its best; it does not need to be fertilized. Yarrow fails where the soil remains wet, and rich soil produces tall, soft stems that may flop and require staking. Mildew can be an issue where summers are hot and humid. Established clumps enlarge and spread; divide every two to three years in fall or early spring. Discard declining parts of any clump; replant vigorous outside parts. Deadhead routinely for further bloom. Yarrow is rabbit and drought resistant, as well as unpalatable to deer.

COMPANION PLANTS

In bloom, the flower heads of yarrow present a horizontal effect. Select upright companions such as rattlesnake master (*Eryngium*

Achillea millefolium comes in many cultivars, including lovely 'Anthea'.

yuccifolium) for architectural contrast. Purple coneflowers (*Echinacea purpurea* and its colorful cultivars), foxglove beardtongue (*Penstemon digitalis*), and wine cups (*Callirhoe involucrata*) combine well with yarrow. Ornamental grasses such as tufted hair grass (*Deschampsia cespitosa*), prairie dropseed (*Sporobolus heterolepis*), and pink muhly grass (*Muhlenbergia capillaris*) also mix well.

DID YOU KNOW?

Achillea gets its name from the legend in Greek mythology that Achilles used the plant to help heal wounded warriors at the Battle of Troy. It has been used medicinally for centuries as a remedy for toothaches and high blood pressure, and to staunch blood flow and close open wounds. The aromatic foliage is dried and placed in closets to protect woolens from clothes moths. Red-banded hairstreak, American copper and other butterflies are attracted to yarrow, along with bees, beetles and flies.

Agastache foeniculum MINT FAMILY (LAMIACEAE)

Anise hyssop, hummingbird mint

DEER RESISTANCE	HARDINESS ZONES	NORTHEAST NATIVE STATES	HEIGHT/SPREAD
9-10	4-8	CT, DE, NH, NY, PA	2-4 FT. × 1½-3 FT.

Agastache 'Blue Boa' is another excellent hybrid cultivar of this plant.

Anise hyssop is a wonderful perennial that is more or less carefree. Its square upright stems are clothed with toothed foliage whose anise fragrance fills the air as you brush by. The fat, showy, poker-like terminal spikes, composed of clusters of tiny, tubular, blue to purplish flowers (called verticillasters), may reach 4 in. in length, but have little or no fragrance. These appear from mid- to late summer. Anise hyssop attracts pollinators that include bees, butterflies, and hummingbirds. It makes a good cut flower and is long-blooming. What more could a gardener ask?

'Blue Fortune' (2-3 ft. × 1½-2 ft.) is a popular cultivar. Its foliage has attractive silvery undersides, and it blooms with 5-in. long spikes of pale blue flower clusters throughout summer and into early fall. This fine perennial is easy to find a place for in most sunny gardens. Other

Agastache foeniculum makes quite a statement in summer.

hybrid cultivars are available on the market, such as *Agastache* 'Blue Boa' (2–3 ft. × 1–1½ ft.), a cultivar of unknown parentage that boasts robust spikes of brilliant, violet-blue flowers for several months, all summer into early fall. Other species of anise hyssop have also proven to be excellent garden performers, as well as pollinator-compatible. Try licorice mint hyssop (*A. rupestris*; 1½–2 ft. × 1–1½ ft.) with its grayish, licorice-scented leaves and loose flower spikes composed of clusters of orange-pink flowers. 'Apache Sunset' (1–2 ft. × 1–1½ ft.) is a very long-blooming selection. All are excellent in beds and borders, as well as in meadows and native plant gardens, cut flower gardens, herb gardens, and elsewhere. These plants are good candidates for mixed containers too.

CULTURE AND TIPS

Well-drained soils and full sun are important for success with anise hyssop. It does best with consistent moisture, but tolerates some drought when established. Routine removal of spent flowers will encourage prolific bloom. Plants tend to seed about, and under good conditions may become aggressive. Increase the sterile hybrid 'Blue Boa' by division or soft stem cuttings in early spring. Rabbits, like deer, tend to avoid these plants.

COMPANION PLANTS

False sunflower (*Heliopsis helianthoides*) and other perennials in the daisy family work well together, including purple coneflower (*Echinacea* species) and yarrow (*Achillea* species).

Agastache 'Blue Fortune' is a popular cultivar of anise hyssop with darker blue or purple flowers.

Rattlesnake master (*Eryngium yuccifolium*) and Mohr's rosinweed (*Silphium mohrii*) are also effective companions. In addition, all five of the native grasses featured in this book work well.

DID YOU KNOW?

This plant's fragrant foliage is a huge deer deterrent, but attractive to people—in fact, its dried foliage is often used as potpourri. Anise hyssop has a variety of culinary uses, including herbal teas and jellies, and its crushed seeds are used as a flavoring. This plant is a hugely successful pollinator-attracting herb; bees, butterflies, and hummingbirds frequently visit for its nectar, especially late in the season when nectar is scarce. Anise hyssop is salt-tolerant, and adapts well to coastal gardens and areas where snow-melting salts are applied in winter.

Allium cernuum ONION FAMILY (ALLIACEAE)

Nodding onion, lady's leek

DEER RESISTANCE	HARDINESS ZONES	NORTHEAST NATIVE STATES	HEIGHT/SPREAD
9-10	4-8	DC, MD, NJ, NY, PA, VA, WV	12-18 IN. × 3-6 IN.

Nodding onion features bluish green, flattened leaves, about 12 in. long, that arise from its base. Bent naked stems (called scapes) are capped by 1- to 2-in. wide umbels, each composed of forty or more flower buds, and ensheathed in a deciduous membrane prior to bloom time. Flowering may last up to two months, from early to late summer, depending upon the weather. Individual flowers are $1/4$ in. across and range in color from pale to dark pink. Heads of seed capsules follow, and once they split open, disseminate their black seeds with abandon.

Carefree nodding onion is appropriate mostly in native plant gardens, meadows, and wild gardens; butterfly and pollinator gardens are also suitable sites. However, it can be used effectively in lightly shaded woodlands, or clustered among perennials in mixed borders and herb gardens.

The foliage and flowers smell oniony only when bruised or cut. Similar prairie onion (*A. stellatum*; 10-14 in. × 8-10 in.) has erect stems with pale to deep lavender-pink, $1/4$-in. flowers arranged in $1^{1}/_{2}$- to 2-in. clusters. The leaves of deep pink Allegheny onion (*A. allegheniensis*; 10-14 in. × 8-10 in.) are used as a substitute for culinary chives.

CULTURE AND TIPS

In the wild, nodding onion is often found growing in sunny places where the soil is poor and thin. It tolerates shallow, rocky soils and droughty conditions, but thrives in average garden soil, dry or damp, even under black walnut trees. To increase stock, start seed in spring, or separate and plant offsets of the bulbs in fall. Deadhead routinely to avoid self-seeding.

COMPANION PLANTS

This plant plays nicely with others, especially native grasses, little bluestem (*Schizachyrium scoparium*) and prairie dropseed (*Sporobolis heterolepis*) in particular. Among other perennials, purple coneflower (*Echinacea purpurea* and its myriad of cultivars) along with Tennessee coneflower (*E. tennesseensis*) make fine companions.

49

Allium cernuum makes a great deer-resistant addition to both sunny and shady spots.

Butterfly flower (*Asclepias tuberosa*), Carolina wild petunia (*Ruellia caroliniensis*), and small-head blazing star (*Liatris microcephala*) are also appropriate.

DID YOU KNOW?

All parts of nodding onions are edible, and were once commonly utilized in soups and stews, although they're seldom found on menus today.

Why do the flower clusters hang down? Some say the flowers nod to keep their pollen dry. Others suggest this drooping habit, which requires upside-down harvesting of pollen and nectar, deters ineffective pollinators, leaving more goodies for efficient bees that don't seem to mind. Butterflies and hummingbirds also visit for the bountiful nectar.

Amsonia tabernaemontana DOGBANE FAMILY (APOCYNACEAE)
Eastern blue star, blue dogbane

DEER RESISTANCE	HARDINESS ZONES	NORTHEAST NATIVE STATES	HEIGHT/SPREAD
9-10	5-8	MD, VA	2-3 FT. × 2-3 FT.

Eastern blue star bears its ³/₄-in. icy blue flowers in pyramid-shaped clusters at the tip of leafy, upright stems in mid-spring. The multiple stems of mature plants grow in an arching habit, forming an attractive vase shape. Its individual ¹/₂- to ³/₄-in., glossy, lance-shaped leaves turn an appealing yellow in fall. Willow-leaved blue star (*A. tabernaemontana* var. *salicifolia*) is quite similar, but has narrower, more delicate foliage, hence its common name.

The cultivar 'Blue Ice' (1-1¹/₂ ft. × 1-1¹/₂ ft.) is thought to be a hybrid with eastern blue star in its parentage, and features very deep blue flowers. 'Storm Cloud' (2-2¹/₂ ft. × 3-3¹/₂ ft.) is noted for its pale flowers on dark, nearly black stems. Downy or fringed blue star (*A. ciliata*) has slightly wider leaves and is somewhat more compact. Its cultivar 'Spring Sky' has larger, longer-lasting flowers than the typical species, but exhibits the same bright fall color.

The cultivar 'Halfway to Arkansas' may be more compact; its foliage is the last of the genus to turn color in fall. Hubricht's blue star (*A. hubrichtii*) is attractive for more than merely the single season it blooms: its showy clusters of pale blue, starry flowers, borne on clumps of strong upright stems, are welcome in mid-spring; numerous, feathery leaves remain attractive through summer. Later on, long, tubular seed-pods develop at the stem tips. In fall, its leaves turn brilliant shades of bright gold that echo the colorful splendor of autumn tree foliage.

All blue stars are easy to grow and very drought-tolerant once established, with the bonus that they make good cut flowers. They are excellent in mixed or perennial beds and borders, and mass well in meadows, wildflower gardens, and among shrubs. They are even effective in large containers, and as shrub-like specimen plants.

Amsonia tabernaemontana flowers in icy blue. Variety *salicifolia*, shown here, features narrower leaves than the species.

CULTURE AND TIPS

Though blue star takes some time to fully mature, it requires little maintenance, and thrives in full sun. In shade, the plant is less floriferous, tends to stretch toward the light, and becomes soft on weak stems. Average garden soil is fine, no need to fertilize—in fact, poor soils render excellent results. Plants grown close to a regularly fertilized and watered lawn will be floppy from excess growth, and will often require staking. Blue star is tolerant of drought because it produces strong taproots as it matures. Once established, this plant resents being divided or transplanted. Propagation is best by seed.

COMPANION PLANTS

Eastern blue star blends well with many plants, especially those with similar cultural requirements. Consider partnering it with blue false indigo (*Baptisia australis*) and its cultivars, including dark-stemmed 'Purple Smoke', or lemon-colored 'Carolina Moonlight'. Lyre-leaf sage (*Salvia lyrata*) makes an excellent underplanting. For a nearly foolproof group, try blue star with false sunflower (*Heliopsis helianthoides*), anise hyssop (*Agastache foeniculum*), and orange coneflower (*Rudbeckia fulgida*) and its cultivars. Native grasses with blue star make an especially stunning combination in autumn.

DID YOU KNOW?

Blue star has a milky, unpalatable sap, and it's this that keeps deer and other herbivores at bay. If stems are harvested for cut flowers, sear the base with a flame immediately after cutting, or dip into boiling water. Either will prevent the sap from fouling vase water. Contact with the sap may cause dermatitis in some people. Blue star is the larval host for caterpillars of the coral hairstreak butterfly. Butterflies, hummingbird moths, and bees (including carpenter bees), are frequent visitors.

Amsonia hubrichtii and *Picea pungens* 'Glauca' offer striking contrast in fall.

Anemone canadensis BUTTERCUP FAMILY (RANUNCULACEAE)

Canada anemone, field anemone

DEER RESISTANCE	HARDINESS ZONES	NORTHEAST NATIVE STATES	HEIGHT/SPREAD
9-10	3-7	CT, MA, MD, ME, NH, NJ, NY, PA, VA, VT, WV	12-24 IN. × 24-30 IN.

Canada anemone is an easy-to-grow species with attractive, deeply-divided foliage and pure white blooms. The 1- to 2-in. wide flowers, composed of five petal-like sepals centered with a boss of yellowish stamens, appear in early summer. These are borne on hairy, 12- to 24-in. stems with one or two tiers of leaves. Spiky, rounded seedheads follow after pollination. Canada anemone is excellent on the edge of woodlands, damp ditches, wildflower gardens, meadows, and as an edging to shrub borders.

Tall thimbleweed (*A. virginiana*), a related species, has three-parted leaves. Its smaller flowers appear midsummer, followed by showy, thimble-shaped, fluffy seedheads that last until fall. Rhizomatous Carolina anemone (*A. caroliniana*; 3-6 in. × 3-6 in.), a diminutive plant native to dry prairies and barrens, is endangered in several states. Its 1- to 1½-in. purple flowers vary quite a bit.

CULTURE AND TIPS

Canada anemone is easy to establish in many garden situations, but in ideal conditions, it can become aggressive. It colonizes rapidly because of fast-growing underground stems and by reseeding. Fall is the best time to divide plants, as well as to direct-sow seed for spring germination. Canada anemone thrives in most types of soils in part sun to part shade, but prefers to remain moist, especially in full sun.

Tall thimbleweed, on the other hand, thrives in dry, rocky places, and tolerates full shade. It provides summertime floral interest to woodlands and native wildflower gardens.

COMPANION PLANTS

Ferns provide foliar contrast with Canada anemone, especially lady fern (*Athyrium filix-femina*) and marginal wood fern (*Dryopteris marginalis*). Wild ginger (*Asarum canadense*) and spreading

Anemone canadensis blooms in early summer in both sun and shade.

sedge (*Carex laxiculmis*) are also attractive companions. In sunnier locations, try combining Canada anemone with shrubs such as summersweet (*Clethra alnifolia*) and winterberry (*Ilex verticillata*).

DID YOU KNOW?

The foliage of Canada anemone and related species contains an unpleasant sap that makes it inedible to deer, rabbits, and other mammals. Native Americans use its roots as a strong natural antiseptic medicine, and it is also used as an astringent to stop bleeding. Sweat bees, mining bees, and small carpenter bees harvest the pollen.

Aquilegia canadensis BUTTERCUP FAMILY (RANUNCULACEAE)

Red columbine, wild columbine

DEER RESISTANCE	HARDINESS ZONES	NORTHEAST NATIVE STATES	HEIGHT/SPREAD
8-10	3-8	CT, DC, DE, MA, MD, ME, NH, NJ, NY, PA, RI, VA, VT, WV	12-36 IN. × 12-18 IN.

The showy flowers of red columbine appear early to mid-spring. Each individual bloom nods, facing downwards from the stem, and is composed of five red outer sepals and five yellow inner petals. Within the yellow petals are the conspicuous anthers and pistil. As flowers fade, seedpods begin to ripen and turn upwards. Once a pod ripens and dries, it splits open lengthwise to release many small black seeds. The thin, "twice-divided-into-three" (or biternate) leaflets may be green or bluish green, and remain attractive after bloom unless marred by leaf miners. Fortunately, this does not affect the health of the plant.

Red columbine is valuable both as a cut flower and a foliage groundcover through the growing season. The compact cultivar 'Little Lanterns' is a diminutive edition of the species and grows only 10 in. or so tall. 'Corbett' has all-yellow flowers on 15- to 18-in. stems. All are appropriate in native, woodland, and wildflower gardens, as well as in open, naturalized places. In beds, borders, and cottage gardens, the flowers offer spring color, and provide nectar for eager hummingbirds early in the season.

CULTURE AND TIPS

Red columbine is easy to grow and naturalizes readily by seed, often appearing in places it wasn't necessarily planted. If saving seed for the following year, be sure to harvest just as the dried seedpods begin to split open. In the wild, columbine occurs in sunny or partly shaded woodlands, in rocky woods with poor, gravelly soils, and on ledges where soil remains moist. Leaf miners often attack red columbine after the plant flowers and goes to seed, boring beneath the outer leaf surfaces, which gives the foliage an unsightly appearance. Refresh affected foliage by cutting it completely to the ground—it will regrow, and rarely be attacked again that year.

COMPANION PLANTS

Complement red columbine with wild bleeding heart (*Dicentra eximia*), early meadow-rue

Aquilegia canadensis blooms profusely in early to mid-spring, and often reseeds.

(*Thalictrum dioicum*), and native wood ferns (*Dryopteris* species). Arrowwood viburnum (*Viburnum dentatum*) and spicebush (*Lindera benzoin*) make excellent woodland shrub companions.

DID YOU KNOW?

Red columbine begins to bloom simultaneously with the return of its most important pollinator, the ruby-throated hummingbird. The relationship is mutually beneficial, as the hummingbird pollinates the plant while it feeds from the nectar-rich flowers. Nectar is located at the tip of each spur, and the hummingbird's long beak and tongue are the perfect setup for accessing it. Red columbine produces copious amounts of pollen, which is an essential source of protein for foraging native bumblebees. Because it is a member of the buttercup family, it contains chemicals that are toxic to herbivores, and therefore the deer will not eat it.

Asarum canadense BIRTHWORT FAMILY (ARISTOLOCHIACEAE)
Wild ginger, Canada wild ginger

DEER RESISTANCE	HARDINESS ZONES	NORTHEAST NATIVE STATES	HEIGHT/SPREAD
9-10	3-7	CT, DC, DE, MA, MD, ME, NH, NJ, NY, PA, RI, VA, VT, WV	4-8 IN. × 12-18 IN.

For an excellent native deer-resistant ground-cover, look no further than wild ginger. Its healthy underground stems colonize slowly to form an impressive mass. Hairy, 6-in. stems bear pairs of deciduous, heart-shaped, matte green leaves, up to 6 in. across, which remain handsome throughout the growing season. Three-pointed, jug-shaped flowers in rusty red, reflexed at the mouth, appear under leaves in mid-spring, so are often overlooked.

Wild ginger works well under many native shrubs and trees as it tolerates a fair amount of shade. Its broad leaves are a perfect contrast to the finer foliage of many other woodland plants.

CULTURE AND TIPS

Select a spot in part to full shade with acidic soil, high in organic matter, that remains consistently moist. Wild ginger can be propagated by three means: dividing the rootstock in autumn, taking rhizome cuttings in summer, and germinating seeds. The latter process requires seed that is freshly harvested from late summer through early fall. Slugs and snails can be a problem, especially to newly emerging plants.

COMPANION PLANTS

Several shade-loving spring wildflowers are natural companions for wild ginger, including wild bleeding heart (*Dicentra eximia*), rue-anemone (*Thalictrum thalictroides*), and red columbine (*Aquilegia canadensis*). For contrasting foliage, combine with seersucker sedge (*Carex plantaginea*) and Appalachian sedge (*Carex appalachica*). Three native ferns to combine with wild ginger are Christmas fern (*Polystichum acrostichoides*), lady fern (*Athyrium filix-femina*), and marginal wood fern (*Dryopteris marginalis*).

Asarum canadense makes an ideal groundcover in partial to full shade.

DID YOU KNOW?

Wild ginger gets its common name from the fact that its rhizomes, when broken, smell exactly like tropical ginger (*Zingiber* species), to which it is not related. This smell is the reason it deters herbivores like rabbits and deer.

Native indigenous people are said to have used wild ginger as a seasoning and an antidote for colds. It is the larval host for caterpillars of the pipeline swallowtail butterfly. Ants are the accepted pollinators, as well as the dispersers of its seed.

59

Asclepias tuberosa MILKWEED FAMILY (ASCLEPIADACEAE)

Butterfly flower, orange milkweed

DEER RESISTANCE	HARDINESS ZONES	NORTHEAST NATIVE STATES	HEIGHT/SPREAD
9-10	3-9	CT, DC, DE, MA, MD, ME, NH, NJ, NY, PA, RI, VA, VT, WV	12-30 IN. × 12-18 IN.

Best known among non-gardeners as the prime attractant for monarch butterflies, butterfly flower grows in sturdy clumps. Its flowers can range in color from deep reddish orange to lemon yellow, but bright orange is typical, and the bloom period is generally from early to mid-summer. Florets are arranged in umbrella-like formations (called umbels) on stiff, upright, or reclining stems that reach up to 36 in. in height. Individual five-parted flowers are complex, with upright horn structures on the petals. Pairs of slightly hairy, lance-shaped leaves are arranged in whorls around the stems.

The cultivar 'Hello Yellow' has heads of bright lemon-yellow flowers; the seed strain 'Gay Butterflies' blooms in a range of red, yellow, and orange. Pale pink flowers of long-blooming showy milkweed (*A. speciosa*; 12-36 in. × 12-18 in.) appear somewhat later than butterfly flower, but it also hosts

caterpillars and provides butterflies with nectar. Swamp milkweed (*A. incarnata*; 48-60 in. × 24-36 in.) is found in the wild in wetlands, and makes an excellent addition to rain gardens and butterfly gardens. Stems bearing pairs of slender leaves are topped by large umbels of vanilla-scented flowers in deep rose. 'Ice Ballet' is a popular cultivar with pure white flowers, as is 'Milkmaid'. 'Soulmate' is cherry pink, whereas 'Cinderella' is dark pink, but with white crowns. Purple milkweed (*A. purpurascens*; 24-36 in. × 12-24 in.) makes large, somewhat aggressive clumps, and may not be appropriate where space is limited.

After bloom time, all species display spindle-shaped seedpods known as follicles, which are useful in dried flower arrangements. The follicles contain numerous, closely packed seeds equipped with feathery, silk-like tails designed especially for wind dispersal.

Asclepias tuberosa brightens the summer garden.

CULTURE AND TIPS

Grow butterfly flower in full sun and well-drained sandy or loamy soil. It tolerates drought well, and makes an excellent addition to gardens that experience dry periods. When grown in rich soils, the result will be overly soft, floppy growth. In the wild, it frequents dry, sandy, or rocky soils, especially in open areas or along roadsides. Butterfly flower freely self-seeds, but seedlings may take two or so years to reach flowering size. Remove seedpods before they ripen and split to avoid excess seeding. Mature milkweed resents being divided or moved because of the potential for taproot damage. Seed is the best approach to effectively increase plants. Germinating in pots and transplanting while young will avoid taproot damage. Be mindful that butterfly flower is late to emerge in spring.

COMPANION PLANTS

Combine butterfly flower with other drought-tolerant plants. Both nodding onion (*Allium cernuum*) and long-blooming spotted beebalm

Look closely and you'll see the intricate arrangement of this butterfly flower's floral parts.

(*Monarda punctata*) provide vertical accent for butterfly flower at bloom time and when the fruits are present; the architectural form of rattlesnake master (*Eryngium yuccifolium*) is another winner. Golden black-eyed Susan (*Rudbeckia hirta*) complements butterfly flower well, but if your color taste runs to magenta and orange, try allowing wine cups (*Callirhoe involucrata*) to scramble through its stems. American star-thistle (*Centaurea americana*) and bearded beggar-ticks (*Bidens aristosa*) make great annual companions.

DID YOU KNOW?

This genus is named for the Greek god of medicine, Asklepios. All species of milkweed serve as host plants for monarch butterfly larvae, and provide the adults with nectar. Perhaps fifty species lay eggs on butterfly flower foliage, including queen butterflies, grey hairstreaks, and milkweed tussock moths. Hummingbirds and bees savor its nectar as well. In times past, the fibrous stems were used to make ropes. Interestingly, butterfly flower is the only species of milkweed without the typical milky sap that gives its family its common name.

Baptisia australis PEA FAMILY (FABACEAE)

Blue false indigo, baptisia

DEER RESISTANCE	HARDINESS ZONES	NORTHEAST NATIVE STATES	HEIGHT/SPREAD
8-10	3-9	CT, DC, MA, MD, NH, NJ, NY, PA, VA, VT, WV	36-48 IN. × 36-48 IN.

Blue false indigo is a splendid native ornamental perennial for most parts of the country. It develops into profuse clumps of attractive, trifoliate, blue-green foliage, above which rise upright spikes of blue pea-like flowers in mid- to late spring, depending on location. Rounded, inflated 2- to 2½-in. seedpods in celadon follow, and turn blackish brown as they age. Known for its deep taproot, baptisia is decidedly drought tolerant once established.

Much breeding work has been done with these plants in recent years, resulting in several hybrids and many cultivated varieties. 'Purple Smoke', with charcoal stems and smoky blue flowers, is popular and similar in size. The white species *B. alba* (24-48 in. × 24-30 in.) and smaller, yellow *B. tinctoria* (24-36 in. × 24-36 in.) are less widely known. Yellow wild indigo (*B. sphaerocarpa*; 24-36 in. × 24-36 in.) brings more yellow flower color into the breeding mix as well, and 'Carolina Moonlight' is a hybrid of it and *B. alba*. Profusely flowering 'Screaming Yellow' is appropriately named; its seedpods are more rounded than those of other species.

The Decadence hybrid series includes gray-stemmed 'Lemon Meringue' (24-36 in. × 24-36 in.), with blue-green leaves and long spikes of yellow flowers, as well as cultivars that are generally shorter and more compact. These include 'Blueberry Sundae', with true blue flowers, and 'Dutch Chocolate', with unusually rich purple-brown flowers above dark blue-green foliage to the base. Bicolored lemon-and-orange 'Solar Flare' is from the Prairies Blues series, also similar in size to the species. All of these are appropriate in beds and borders, among shrubs, naturalized in meadows and native plant gardens, as well as butterfly gardens. The compact forms are especially prized for small gardens.

CULTURE AND TIPS

Baptisia thrives in full sun with well-drained soil, and also tolerates poor soil. If grown in too rich a soil and too much shade, the plant will be taller, bloom less, and tend to need staking. It resents being divided and transplanted because of its deep, extensive roots. Increasing plants is best accomplished by purchasing young potted

Baptisia australis brings stunning verticality to the garden with brilliant blue flowers.

plants, or by seed, though plants from seed take several years to flower. Grow seed in containers for the first year, transplanting carefully so the taproot can establish. Cuttings of soft, young shoots taken in spring and treated with rooting hormone are usually successful. Keep young plants watered well. Some gardeners clip off the seedpods as they develop to use the foliage mass as a shrub substitute, but the attractiveness of the pods is lost as a result of this practice. Pests and diseases are rare in this plant.

COMPANION PLANTS

Try *B. australis* with the cultivar 'Screaming Yellow', or its cousin *B. sphaerocarpa*. Rattlesnake master (*Eryngium yuccifolium*) provides contrast in texture and form. Ornamental grasses, including *Panicum virgatum* 'Cloud Nine', 'Northwind',

and 'Dallas Blues', are good companions, especially in meadows. Other herbaceous, sun-loving companions are wild bergamot (*Monarda fistulosa*), especially the cultivar 'Claire Grace', and 'Prairie Splendor' purple coneflower (*Echinacea purpurea*). In annuals, star-thistle (*Centaurea americana*) makes an excellent choice.

DID YOU KNOW?

Baptisia australis was named the perennial plant of the year for 2010 by the Perennial Plant Association, and is a host plant for wild indigo duskywing butterflies. In times gone by, mothers cut the black seedpods and gave them to children to play with as rattles. Blue false indigo was used to produce dyes years ago, though it rendered inferior results, and has been replaced by much more effective products.

Callirhoe involucrata MALLOW FAMILY (MALVACEAE)

Wine cups, purple poppy mallow

DEER RESISTANCE	HARDINESS ZONES	NORTHEAST NATIVE STATES	HEIGHT/SPREAD
8-10	4-8	PA, VA	8-12 IN. × 24-36 IN.

Wine cups is a common name that describes this plant perfectly, with its chalice-like 1- to 1½-in. wide blooms in brilliant magenta, ringed with bracts; each flower's five petals has a white spot at the base. Solitary flowers face the sky, opening in the morning and closing at night. Long axillary stems rise from a sizable taproot and sprawl along the ground, forming thick mats. Grayish green leaves are deeply lobed in the shape of hands.

This showy, long-blooming perennial is perfect for trailing over walls, and as a wide-spreading groundcover. It thrives in sunny rock gardens, and as a component in pollinator and native plant gardens. Bush's poppy mallow (*Callirhoe bushii*) is less common in the marketplace. Its stems sprawl, but less so than wine cups, and bear magenta blooms like miniature hollyhock flowers for much of summer.

CULTURE AND TIPS

In the wild, wine cups grows in dry, open places in full sun. In the garden, find a sunny spot where soil drains well. The long taproot means it tolerates drought readily, but resents being moved or divided. Propagation is easily achieved by sowing seed, but also from vegetative cuttings of young growth in spring. Deadhead routinely to extend bloom time. Protect plants from slug damage; rust sometimes attacks the foliage in wet seasons.

COMPANION PLANTS

This plant's trailing habit and strongly lobed, pubescent foliage are especially attractive when planted with contrasting shapes and leaf textures of other plants. Grasses such as prairie dropseed (*Sporobolus heterolepis*) and muhly grass (*Muhlenbergia capillaris*) provide

Callirhoe involucrata features deep magenta flowers, and thrives in difficult spots in full sun.

an effective contrast in foliage. Pair it with pink smallhead blazing star (*Liatris microcephala*), orange butterfly flower (*Asclepias tuberosa*), or plains tickseed (*Coreopsis tinctoria*) and bearded beggar-ticks (*Bidens aristosa*) for floral interest.

DID YOU KNOW?

Wine cups has been used as a medicinal plant for generations, particularly to reduce pain. The flowers attract numerous native butterflies and bees for nectar, especially bumblebees. It is an important host plant for gray hairstreak caterpillars.

Chrysogonum virginianum DAISY FAMILY (ASTERACEAE)

Green-and-gold, goldenstar

DEER RESISTANCE	HARDINESS ZONES	NORTHEAST NATIVE STATES	HEIGHT/SPREAD
7-10	5-9	DC, MD, NY, PA, VA, WV	$1/2$-12 IN. × $3/4$-18 IN.

Green-and-gold features fuzzy, oval leaves on pubescent stems that trail along the ground and root at each node, thereby making it an effective groundcover. In spring, numerous 1- to $1^{1}/_{2}$-in. blooms in bright yellow appear on hairy stems above the green foliage; often they appear again when temperatures cool in autumn. Each flower is composed of five yellow ray petals, each minutely notched at the tip, surrounding a central cluster of short stamens.

Several cultivars are available, including 'Eco-Lacquered Spider', a dependable spreader. 'Pierre' spreads less assertively, and reportedly tolerates drier conditions better than the species. 'Superstar' (formerly known as 'Norman Singer Form') tends to create smaller clumps rather than spreading. 'Allen Bush' is a compact, dwarf cultivar that is also suitable for containers. All cultivars feature similar flower form and color.

CULTURE AND TIPS

Green-and-gold does best in part shade, and puts on an excellent display where soil is consistently moist, acidic, and high in organic matter. Poorly drained sites can cause fungal problems. Do not bury its crowns with mulch or leaf litter. Under excellent conditions, its rhizomes can become assertive, so keep that in mind when siting it in the garden. Green-and-gold responds well to cutbacks, and will regrow readily. Propagate easily by division any time during the growing season, but keep well watered until established.

COMPANION PLANTS

Green-and-gold's low habit offers a perfect ground-level tableau for contrasting taller plants. The distinctive foliage of Christmas fern (*Polystichum acrostichoides*), celandine poppy (*Stylophorum diphyllum*), and Jacob's

Chrysogonum virginianum is well suited as a groundcover in part sun to shade.

ladder (*Polemonium reptans*) provides textural contrast with green-and-gold over many months. In spring, wild bleeding heart (*Dicentra eximia*) is a colorful companion, along with rue-anemone (*Thalictrum thalictroides*). For early summer, consider the vibrant blooms of Indian pink (*Spigelia marilandica*) to provide height at the back of the border. Spreading sedge (*Carex laxiculmis*) and seersucker sedge (*Carex plantaginea*) are excellent choices to complement masses of green-and-gold. Allegheny serviceberry (*Amelanchier laevis*) makes a perfect shrubby accompaniment.

DID YOU KNOW?

Bees are attracted to green-and-gold's open flowers for pollen and nectar, both early and late in the year. The seeds are favorites of songbirds and ground-feeding birds in fall.

Conoclinium coelestinum DAISY FAMILY (ASTERACEAE)

Blue mistflower, wild ageratum

DEER RESISTANCE
7-10

HARDINESS ZONES
5-10

NORTHEAST NATIVE STATES
DC, DE, MD, NJ, NY, PA, VA, WV

HEIGHT/SPREAD
18-36 IN. × 18-36 IN.

A distant cousin to the popular annual ageratum, blue mistflower is a true perennial. Supported by green- or purple-flushed, branching stems, its fluffy, flat-topped, lavender flowers put on a show from summer well into fall. Individual florets lack the ray petals that characterize most members of the daisy family, but they produce copious amounts of nectar that attracts wildlife—a valuable food source during late summer in butterfly and pollinator gardens. Toothed leaves occur in pairs up the stems. Blue mistflower is excellent massed as a tall groundcover in moist meadows and naturalized places, or in cut flower and rain gardens.

CULTURE AND TIPS

Site blue mistflower in full sun to part shade, where there is consistent moisture and the soil is high in organic matter. This species tolerates wet places. If happy, it can become aggressive by means of spreading rhizomes, and will need control. Plan accordingly and site it where it can spread out freely, and show its copious display of flowers. Dig out unwanted rhizomes and deadhead routinely to prevent self-seeding. Divide clumps in spring once growth emerges, or increase by soft cuttings of young growth. Seed also germinates readily, and may be sown directly outdoors after spring frosts or in fall. When grown by itself, blue mistflower often needs staking, and it benefits from stronger-stemmed companions as neighbors, especially in windy areas. In small gardens, or where space is limited, control its assertive tendencies by planting in sunken containers, and by pruning heavily early in the season to keep it in scale. Blue mistflower makes an excellent, long-lasting cut flower, and adds a cool color to otherwise warmly hued summer flower arrangements.

COMPANION PLANTS

Blue mistflower is best sited in a more natural garden setting. Try providing it with a

Conoclinium coelestinum makes a statement in late summer, with purple flowers that last weeks on end.

background of shrubs, including spicebush (*Lindera benzoin*) or red-osier dogwood (*Cornus sericea*). Coupled with blue mistflower, the latter's clusters of white flowers in spring, bird-attracting bluish white berries in fall, and red-barked stems in winter provide for visual interest year-round. Since this plant thrives in wet areas, try red cardinal flower (*Lobelia cardinalis*) as a striking accompaniment. Swamp milkweed (*Asclepias incarnata*), New York ironweed (*Vernonia novaboracensis*), and fetterbush (*Eubotrys racemosus*) are also outstanding companions.

DID YOU KNOW?

Blue mistflower is popular with many species of butterflies, including skippers, queens, swallowtails, and pearly crescents. Monarchs rely on this plant during their migration south toward the end of the season, when nectar is in short supply. From late summer on, various insects that feed on the plant's foliage provide food for bluebirds, orioles, and redwing blackbirds, among others.

Coreopsis pubescens DAISY FAMILY (ASTERACEAE)
Star tickseed, downy tickseed

DEER RESISTANCE	HARDINESS ZONES	NORTHEAST NATIVE STATES	HEIGHT/SPREAD
8-10	6-9	CT, MA, VA, WV	24-48 IN. × 18-30 IN.

Another tried-and-true and highly recommended native perennial is the star tickseed (*Coreopsis pubescens*). Its 2-in. flower heads have irregularly notched ray florets in bright yellow, centered with disk flowers in darker yellow, and occasionally yellow-orange. The blooms make a splash in sunny places from early to midsummer and on into early fall. Stems and dark green, lance-shaped leaves are covered with downy hairs.

A clumping, low-maintenance perennial, this plant is a fitting component of dry meadows and naturalized areas, as well as pollinator and butterfly gardens. It tolerates drought, humidity, and high temperatures without missing a beat, and makes an excellent, long-lasting cut flower.

The compact and free-blooming cultivar 'Sunshine Superman' (9-12 in. × 6-9 in.) is perfect for inclusion in small gardens. It also self-seeds freely, and is appropriate as a groundcover in dry, sunny places, in containers, and as an edging at the front of dry beds and borders. Similar species of this genus are also popular for sunny gardens. Dwarf tickseed (*C. auriculata*; 12-18 in. × 12-18 in.) spreads by rhizomes, and is perfect for smaller spaces. The cultivar 'Nana'

(6-9 in. × 6-9 in.) is especially valuable for containers, mass plantings, and as a groundcover, as well as for edging. 'Zamphir' (10-15 in. × 12-18 in.) has fluted, orange-petaled flowers, and 'Jethro Tull' (12-18 in. × 12-18 in.) is considered an improved hybrid. Large-flowered tickseed, or common coreopsis (*C. grandiflora*), and lanceleaf coreopsis (*C. lanceolata*) are clump-forming (both 18-24 in. × 18-24 in.) with bright yellow 1- to 2-in. wide flower heads. 'Baby Sun' ('Sonnenkind'; 12-18 in. × 12-15 in.) is a compact cultivar of lanceleaf coreopsis. The hybrid 'Early Sunrise' (18-24 in. × 18-24 in.) has semi-double, 2- to 3-in. blooms in mid- to late summer. Deadheading helps prolong its bloom period—it also makes a fine cut flower. Tall tickseed (*C. tripteris*; 24-96 in. × 24-96 in.) is a bold addition for the back of large borders, or meadows where soil is dry and poor.

CULTURE AND TIPS

Best in full sun, star tickseed will also persist with half-day sun. Provide average, well-drained, or even thin, dry soil; wet feet and poor drainage will quickly bring about its demise. Deadhead routinely to extend flowering and reduce self-seeding. If plants start to sprawl,

Coreopsis pubescens is a dependable summer perennial, and one of the many species of tickseed deer don't find palatable.

don't hesitate to cut them back hard to promote bushiness and later bloom. This task also promotes good air circulation and deters outbreaks of powdery mildew, which sometimes attacks the foliage. Tickseeds are typically short-lived perennials, and benefit from division every two to three years to maintain vigor. Alternatively, start new plants in situ from seed, or transplant self-seeded ones.

COMPANION PLANTS

The blue-flowered spikes of anise hyssop (*Agastache foeniculum*) make fine vertical contrast for the sunny, daisy-like flowers of star tickseed, while those of annual star-thistle (*Centaurea americana*) repeat its form in pink. In meadows, native ornamental grasses such as pink muhly grass (*Muhlenbergia capillaris*) and prairie dropseed (*Sporobolus heterolepis*) are attractive companions. Echo the golden flowers with annual sneezeweed (*Helenium amarum*), yellow coneflower (*Echinacea paradoxa*), or even tall cut-leaved coneflower (*Rudbeckia laciniata*). For a monochromatic theme, try Maryland senna (*Senna marilandica*), which brings contrasting foliage and long clusters of bright yellow pea flowers. Allegheny serviceberry (*Amelanchier laevis*) is an ideal shrubby companion.

DID YOU KNOW?

The specific name *pubescens* refers to the downy hairs that clothe the stems and leaves of this plant. This hairiness, also known as pubescence, is a general deterrent to deer herbivory. Several butterflies visit star tickseed and other *Coreopsis* species for nectar, including monarchs and common buckeyes, as well as countless bumblebees in search of pollen.

Dicentra eximia FUMITORY FAMILY (FUMARIACEAE)

Wild bleeding heart, fringed bleeding heart

DEER RESISTANCE	HARDINESS ZONES	NORTHEAST NATIVE STATES	HEIGHT/SPREAD
9-10	3-9	MA, MD, NJ, NY, PA, VA, VT, WV	9-24 IN. × 18 IN.

Dicentra eximia is effective singly or in groups.

Wild bleeding heart is a popular native perennial of shaded or partly shaded ornamental gardens, for its fern-like dissected foliage as well as its graceful clusters of dangling, heart-shaped flowers in a spectrum of pink. From late spring and sporadically through the season, these flowers rise above upright mounds of foliage, often on pinkish stems.

'Luxuriant' is a cultivar that tolerates heat and sunnier spots more than others, and is thought to be a hybrid of the species addressed here and western bleeding heart (*Dicentra formosa*). There is also a naturally occurring pure white flower variant, 'Alba', with pale green stems. The plant's pale, blue-green, deeply cut leaves grow from the base, and foliage persists after bloom, unlike those of the plant's similar, ephemeral spring cousins, squirrel corn (*D. canadensis*) and Dutchman's breeches (*D. cucullaria*).

White-flowered squirrel corn (3-5 in. × 8-12 in.) is occasionally used as an ornamental, and bears fewer flowers, which are short-lived but fragrant. Its common name refers to its yellow tubers, which appear similar to kernels of corn. Dutchman's breeches (6-12 in. × 6-12 in.) blooms before the trees leaf out in woodlands, and its white flowers resemble upside-down pantaloons, hence its common name.

A valuable accompaniment to other shade lovers, wild bleeding heart is ideal beneath shrubs, or to enliven sheltered beds and borders, and as edging or groundcover in the naturalistic garden.

CULTURE AND TIPS

Site wild bleeding heart in partly shaded spots. Too much shade results in sparse bloom; full sun is only appropriate if soil can be kept moist throughout summer. Organically rich soil that drains well is ideal; in poorly drained soil, plants will fall prey to crown rot. If necessary, amend the soil with well-rotted compost or other organic material prior to spring planting. Deadhead to the crown as needed to prevent self-seeding and encourage repeat bloom. If any foliage yellows and becomes shabby in hot weather, refresh it by cutting it back to the crown, a practice that encourages new growth. Increase stock by dividing established plants after flowering. Plants grow readily from directly sown fresh seed.

COMPANION PLANTS

Choose companions for wild bleeding heart that will emphasize both its lovely foliage and floral attributes. Try it with wild ginger (*Asarum canadense*), Jacob's ladder (*Polemonium reptans*), celandine poppy (*Stylophorum diphyllum*), and Canada anemone (*Anemone canadensis*) to create a tapestry in shade. Green-and-gold (*Chrysogonum virginianum*) would be beautiful with both the pink and white-flowered forms.

DID YOU KNOW?

Wild bleeding heart's pollen-loaded flowers attract native bees and honeybees, especially early and late in the season, when pollen may be scarce. Hummingbirds are frequent visitors for nectar, and are probably the primary pollinators. The plant is spread by ants—a trait known as myrmecochory—which feed on the white, fleshy structures attached to its seeds. These are called eliasomes, and they contain rich lipids and proteins ants love. The ants, in turn, distribute the seeds when they take them back to their nests underground.

Flowers of wild bleeding heart are held just above ferny foliage in mid-spring, and sporadically throughout summer.

Echinacea purpurea DAISY FAMILY (ASTERACEAE)

Purple coneflower, eastern purple coneflower

DEER RESISTANCE	HARDINESS ZONES	NORTHEAST NATIVE STATES	HEIGHT/SPREAD
7-9	3-8	CT, MD, NJ, NY, PA, VA, WV	24-60 IN. × 18-24 IN.

This tried-and-true perennial has become one of the most recognizable native garden plants. Considered by many to be an icon of prairies, purple coneflower blooms from late spring for weeks on end. Its flower heads are attractive, each with slightly drooping, purple ray petals centered on a brown, spiny, cone-shaped disk. The flower heads occur atop coarse, bristly stems, both branched and unbranched. Lance-shaped foliage is dark green, and also bristly.

Others in the genus include the more compact narrow-leaf coneflower (*E. angustifolia*; 12-24 in. × 8-18 in.), with light pink or purple ray petals that point sideways and down, and pale purple coneflower (*E. pallida*; 24-36 in. × 12-18 in.), which has narrow ray petals that point decidedly downward. Yellow coneflower (*E. paradoxa*; 24-36 in. × 12-18 in.) has greenish brown cones with drooping ray petals in lemon yellow. All have been the subject of extensive breeding programs, resulting in a plethora of selections, cultivars, and hybrids in the marketplace. Bloom color ranges from various shades of white, pink, purple, red, and maroon to yellow, gold, bronze, and even green. Bicolored forms also exist, like the purple and green cultivar 'Twister'. Simple, single flower heads, some as large as 6 in. across, as well as semi-doubles and fully-doubles, have captured the imagination of gardeners across the nation.

Excellent as a cut flower and in containers, coneflower is appropriate massed in meadows, native plant, pollinator, and butterfly gardens, and as a backdrop in beds and borders.

Echinacea purpurea is one of our finest native perennials, and never fails to make a gorgeous garden addition.

CULTURE AND TIPS

Coneflower thrives in full sun in average soils that drain well—avoid poorly drained or wet soils. Its tolerance of drought, humidity, poor soil, and high temperatures makes it an excellent candidate for all sorts of garden situations. Pests and diseases are relatively few, and the plant requires little maintenance once established. Japanese beetles may occasionally eat the petals. Deadheading spent flower heads will often encourage further blooming, but remember that many seed-eating birds depend on this plant as a food source, especially late in the season. Increase and maintain plants' vigor by dividing clumps in spring or fall every few years. Water well until established—good practice in general, and one that hugely benefits flower production. The species and some selections can be started from seed, but many are sterile. Be aware that many of the semi-double

The name *Echinacea* is derived from the Greek word for hedgehog, a reference to the flower's spiny center.

and fully double forms have no central cone and do not produce seed, thus they have no benefits to bees or seed-eating birds like the single forms do.

COMPANION PLANTS

In prairies or meadows, it's hard to beat ornamental grasses as companions. Try a selection of little bluestem (*Schizachyrium scoparium* 'Standing Ovation' or 'The Blues'), as well as prairie dropseed (*Sporobolus heterolepis*). Pink muhly grass (*Muhlenbergia capillaris*) is another outstanding choice, with its misty, late summer display of bright pink flowers. Position it behind a stand of purple coneflowers, where in early fall, the sun will shine through the grass, silhouetting the flower cones. For flower contrast, the purple-blue flowers of anise hyssop (*Agastache foeniculum*), azure blue sage

(*Salvia azurea* var. *grandiflora*), and dense blazing star (*Liatris spicata*) work well in meadows and flowerbeds alike.

DID YOU KNOW?

Derived from the Greek *echino*, meaning hedgehog, the botanical name *Echinacea* alludes to the spiny central disk of this plant's flower heads. Native Americans found medicinal value in all parts of the plant, and today, *Echinacea* has become one of the most widely used herbs for an array of ailments, particularly to boost the immune system. Its flower heads attract butterflies such as painted ladies, fritillaries, and swallowtails, along with many types of native bees in search of nectar. Ruby-throated hummingbirds also feed upon the flowers' nectar. Goldfinches and other seed-eating birds feast on seed from late summer into early fall.

Eryngium yuccifolium PARSLEY FAMILY (APIACEAE)

Rattlesnake master, button snakeroot

DEER RESISTANCE	HARDINESS ZONES	NORTHEAST NATIVE STATES	HEIGHT/SPREAD
9-10	3-8	CT, MD, NJ, VA	48-60 IN. × 24-36 IN.

Valued as much for its bold, architectural habit as for its unique flower heads, rattlesnake master stands out in residential beds and meadows. Bold clumps of gray-green, sword-shaped basal leaves, each 2 to 3 ft. long, resemble foliage of spine-tipped *Yucca*, hence the plant's specific name. A beefy rootstock gives rise to one or more stiff, smooth stems, each bearing a few spikey leaves and topped with branched clusters of prickly, 1-in. wide, egg-shaped or rounded flower heads. These heads are composed of densely packed umbels of fragrant, tiny white flowers.

Bloom occurs in midsummer, and flower stalks are very long lasting, persisting until late fall. Use rattlesnake master for height and vertical structure. The flower heads are popular as cut flowers, both fresh and dried. This unusual native is memorable in wild gardens, meadows, pollinator, and native plant gardens, as well as among other perennials in beds and borders.

It is considered a signature plant of the tallgrass prairie. A cultivar called 'Kershaw Blue' features powder blue foliage.

CULTURE AND TIPS

Rattlesnake master, which is drought-tolerant once established, must be grown in full sun with average, well-drained soil for good results. As long as drainage is good, difficult soils like clay, gravel, and even those that are shallow and rocky are acceptable. Overly rich soil results in weak stems that often flop. Sometimes rabbits attack the soft, young growth. Toward the end of the season, remove any stems that have flopped to the base to curtail self-seeding. If left for winter interest, the flower heads provide food for seed-eating birds, especially finches.

COMPANION PLANTS

An excellent native grass choice is switchgrass (*Panicum virgatum*) and its cultivars,

Eryngium yuccifolium brings a unique look and structure to the deer-resistant perennial garden.

like metallic blue 'Heavy Metal' and upright 'Northwind', which provide an effective foliage contrast to rattlesnake master. Other perennials that mix well include Carolina wild petunia (*Ruellia caroliniensis*), smallhead blazing star (*Liatris microcephala*), and butterfly flower (*Asclepias tuberosa*). Don't forget annual and biennial companions like brown-eyed Susan (*Rudbeckia triloba*) and sneezeweed (*Helenium amarum*).

DID YOU KNOW?

History recounts that a tea was made from the roots of this plant and given to victims of rattlesnake bites, hence its common name. Purportedly, baskets and sandals were crafted from its fibrous leaves. Rattlesnake master provides nectar for a huge range of insects. Use it to attract monarchs and other butterflies to the garden, though wasps, bees, and flies are its primary pollinators.

Eutrochium maculatum DAISY FAMILY (ASTERACEAE)
Spotted Joe-Pye weed

DEER RESISTANCE
8–9

HARDINESS ZONES
4–9

NORTHEAST NATIVE STATES
CT, MA, MD, ME, NH, NJ, NY, PA, RI, VA, VT, WV

HEIGHT/SPREAD
4–7 FT. × 3–4 FT.

Though the common name of Joe-Pye "weed" may suggest otherwise, this native plant is an excellent addition to many a sunny garden. Sturdy stems are dotted with dark maroon, and feature whorls of four or five lance-shaped leaves rimmed with small teeth. Loose, flat-topped, light purple flower heads are composed of disk flowers, and are delightfully fragrant—they also make excellent cut flowers. Joe-Pye weed's grand stature and huge, mounded clusters of flowers are especially valuable mid- to late summer. It brings height and architectural interest to a variety of settings, especially in informal plantings. Try it among shrubs, at the back of residential beds and borders, in sunny meadows, or wildflower gardens. It is also known as *Eupatorium maculatum*.

Spotted Joe-Pye weed puts on a midsummer show.

81

Not to be overlooked is related sweet Joe-Pye weed (*E. purpureum*; 4–7 ft. × 2–4 ft.), which sports fluffy, dome-shaped inflorescences of lavender-pink flowers that may reach 10 in. or more across, and aromatic leaves. The cultivar 'Bartered Bride' (6–10 ft. × 4–6 ft.) is off-white in color, while recently introduced 'Joe White' (6–7 ft. × 3–5 ft.) comes in bright white. A compact cultivar called 'Gateway' (4–5 ft. × 1½–2 ft.), often listed as *E. purpureum* ssp. *maculatum* 'Gateway', has become popular for its oversized, densely packed clusters of pale ruby flowers on burgundy-colored stems. Often 'Little Joe' (3–4 ft. × 1–3 ft.) and 'Baby Joe' (2–3 ft. × 1–2 ft.) are attributed to spotted Joe-Pye weed, but these cultivars actually belong to coastal plain Joe-Pye weed (*E. dubium*; 2–5 ft. × 1½–2 ft.), and they will grow in more shade. 'Purple Bush' (4½–5½ ft. × 2–4 ft.) and 'Phantom' (2–4 ft. × 1–2 ft.) are other recommended cultivars on the market.

CULTURE AND TIPS

Spotted Joe-Pye weed does best in full sun to part shade where soil is fertile and consistently moist. It does not accept drought, but tolerates clay and wet soils. Leave plants standing for winter interest, but cut them down before winter's end to make way for spring growth. Increase by cuttings of soft new growth, or divide in spring or fall. Seed also germinates readily. Powdery mildew may be an issue; however, it does not affect the plant's performance in the garden. Joe-Pye weed species and cultivars are generally pest resistant, but they do host native leaf beetles and several species of moth caterpillars, so any damage to the leaves is yet another important facet of their ecological role.

COMPANION PLANTS

Select moisture-tolerant companions for Joe-Pye weed. Try it in a rain garden with cardinal flower (*Lobelia cardinalis*) and any of its cultivars, such as 'Black Truffle', 'Fried Green Tomatoes', or 'New Moon Maroon'. Other compatible native perennials include swamp milkweed (*Asclepias incarnata*), wild bergamot (*Monarda fistulosa*), and New York ironweed (*Vernonia noveboracensis*). Add the shrub black chokeberry (*Aronia melanocarpa*) for structure and to mitigate erosion. Summersweet (*Clethra alnifolia*) and Virginia sweetspire (*Itea virginica*) are also excellent companions.

DID YOU KNOW?

Who was Joe Pye? The story goes that he was an 18th-century herbalist or medicine man who used this plant as an antidote for typhus fever. His namesake plant also tolerates growing conditions near black walnut trees, which secrete a compound called juglone from their roots that affects many plants negatively. It is an ecologically important source of nectar, attracting butterflies like monarchs, tiger swallowtails, variegated fritillaries, red admirals, and spotted purples, not to mention many moths and native bumblebees.

Eutrochium maculatum is one of several species of Joe-Pye weed that are both bountiful and ecologically important.

Helenium autumnale DAISY FAMILY (ASTERACEAE)

Common sneezeweed, Helen's flower

DEER RESISTANCE	HARDINESS ZONES	NORTHEAST NATIVE STATES	HEIGHT/SPREAD
8-10	3-8	CT, DC, DE, MA, MD, NJ, NY, PA, RI, VA, VT, WV	36-60 IN. × 24-36 IN.

People with allergies to wind-pollinated plants have little reason to worry about growing perennial sneezeweed, for insects, not wind, disseminate its heavy, waxy pollen. Clumps of this easy-to-grow plant bloom mid- to late summer and continue into fall. Winged, branching stems carry 4- to 6- in. long, ovate leaves, and are topped with groups of daisy-like 2-in. flower heads. Triangular, bright yellow ray petals, three-lobed at their tips, are centered with greenish yellow disk flowers.

Common sneezeweed is appropriate for rain gardens, waterside gardens, excellent in cottage gardens, and does well in mixed or perennial borders in more formal settings. Numerous cultivars are available, including the best known, early-blooming copper red-flowered 'Moerheim Beauty' (22-36 in. × 12-18 in.). Midsummer-blooming 'Pumilum Magnificum' (24-36 in. × 24-36 in.) and later-blooming 'Butterpat' (36-48 in. × 18-24 in.) are beautiful clear yellows. Midseason 'Bruno' (38-42 in. × 18-24 in.) blooms with deep red-brown heads with brown disks. Common sneezeweed is an excellent, long-lasting cut flower.

CULTURE AND TIPS

Perennial common sneezeweed thrives in full sun to part shade where the soil is average to wet, and consistent moisture is especially important in summer. Deadhead spent flowers routinely for extended bloom. To keep the plants shorter than the usual 36 to 60 in., pinch the stem tips back when young plants reach 6 to 8 in. tall; or later, in mid-July, cut plants back by about one-third to one-half their height. These operations encourage bushy growth with plenty of flowers. Divide clumps every two to three

Helenium autumnale is available in many cultivars in a range of colors. Shown here is 'Moerheim Beauty'.

years in spring or fall to maintain vigor, and to increase stock. Though powdery mildew may appear on the foliage, it does not affect the plants' performance.

COMPANION PLANTS

Partner sneezeweed with others that prefer moist soil, such as purplish or white dense blazing star (*Liatris spicata*), and shrubs like fetterbush (*Eubotrys racemosus*) and red-osier dogwood (*Cornus sericea*). Other companions might include pink-purple swamp milkweed (*Asclepias incarnata*), yellow Maryland senna (*Senna marilandica*), and red cardinal flower (*Lobelia cardinalis*).

DID YOU KNOW?

The leaves and disk flowers of sneezeweed were once processed and used as a substitute for snuff, hence its common name. Red admirals and other butterflies, flies, and bees are frequent visitors to its flowers, especially late in the season when food is less plentiful.

Heliopsis helianthoides   DAISY FAMILY (ASTERACEAE)

False sunflower, oxeye sunflower

DEER RESISTANCE	HARDINESS ZONES	NORTHEAST NATIVE STATES	HEIGHT/SPREAD
9-10	3-9	CT, DC, DE, MA, MD, ME, NH, NJ, NY, PA, RI, VA, VT, WV	4-6 FT. × 2-4 FT.

False sunflower features clumps of sturdy, tough-branched stems furnished with pairs of coarse, oval, bristly leaves, rimmed with pointed teeth and 3 to 6 in. long. This plant's upright, brilliant lemon yellow flower heads, up to 3 in. across, consist of both ray and disk florets, both of which are fertile and able to produce seed. Bloom season lasts from early to late summer; flowers are prized by butterflies and pollinating insects, while gardeners prize the flowers for cutting and for feeding those pollinators. A member of the vast daisy family, it is closely related to true sunflowers and rosinweeds. Many of these native sunflower-like perennials grew wild on North America's once-boundless tallgrass prairies, before agriculture claimed much of that land.

More than a few excellent cultivars are on the market, including compact, orange-centered 'Tuscan Sun' (2-3 ft. × 1½-2 ft.), and 'Prairie Sunset' (4-5 ft. × 1½-2 ft.) with dark purple stems and purple-veined leaves. Double-flowered cultivars include 'Double Sunstruck' (14-16 in. × 12-14 in.) and 'Asahi' (2-2½ ft. × 1½-2 ft.), with golden yellow pompon-like flower heads atop branching stems. The variety *Heliopsis helianthoides* var. *scabra* (which means rough) gave rise to several outstanding cultivated varieties: 'Burning Hearts' (3-4ft. × 1-1½ft.) is a showstopper with its bicolored bright yellow, orange-centered ray flowers and purple foliage; 'Summer Sun' (also known as 'Sommersonne'; 3-4 ft. × 1½-2 ft.) is popular with its semi-double golden ray petals and variegated cream-and-green foliage. Variegated 'Sunburst' and similar 'Helhan' ('Loraine Sunshine') are also popular. All are excellent in sunny beds and borders, and for their important ecological role in naturalized wildlife gardens, where they not only provide nectar and pollen for pollinators in summer, but also seed for songbirds in fall, and overwintering sites for beneficial insects.

Heliopsis helianthoides puts on a lovely midsummer show.

CULTURE AND TIPS

Plant false sunflower in average soil in full sun, preferably in well-drained soil. Although it tolerates drought, it does best if supplied with water during dry periods. Plants flower less and tend to be much less vigorous in poor, infertile soils, and most species do not handle shade well. To control height for tall selections, cut developing stems by about a third in late spring, or stake to prevent occasional flopping. Routine deadheading encourages extended bloom. Increase plants by division in fall, or soft cuttings in spring. Start seed indoors in fall or winter, or in spring at 60-70°F. Aphids and powdery mildew may sometimes be an issue, but false sunflower is seldom bothered by pests and diseases. Thin out overly dense plants to improve air flow, which helps reduce the chance of mildew.

COMPANION PLANTS

Many perennials are suitable companions for false sunflower. Try beebalm (*Monarda fistulosa*), sweet Joe-Pye weed (*Eutrochium purpureum*), and common sneezeweed (*Helenium autumnale*). Native grasses such as prairie dropseed (*Sporobolus heterolepis*) and switchgrass

Heliopsis helianthoides 'Bleeding Hearts' brings a deep orange glow to the summer garden.

(*Panicum virgatum*) also combine well. Consider a combination planting of false sunflower with shrubby St. John's wort (*Hypericum prolificum*) and switchgrass cultivars like 'Dallas Blues' and 'Heavy Metal'. Two other recommended shrub companions are red chokeberry (*Aronia arbutifolia*) and northern bayberry (*Morella pensylvanica*).

DID YOU KNOW?

Helianthoides, this plant's species name, means "*Helianthus*-like" in Latin, because it closely resembles the genus of the true sunflowers, *Helianthus*. Many butterflies, such as red admirals, skippers, crescents, and common ringlets are attracted to its flowers, which are rich in nectar. Hummingbirds, ground beetles, and soldier beetles also come to feed, while green sweat bees, small carpenter bees, and bumblebees collect pollen. Songbirds happily harvest the seed as soon as it ripens.

Iris versicolor   IRIS FAMILY (IRIDACEAE)

Northern blue flag, blue flag

DEER RESISTANCE	HARDINESS ZONES	NORTHEAST NATIVE STATES	HEIGHT/SPREAD
9-10	3-9	CT, DC, DE, MA, MD, ME, NH, NJ, NY, PA, RI, VA, VT	24-30 IN. × 24-30 IN.

The intricate, 4-in. wide flowers of northern blue flag rise above clumps of long, sword-like leaves in late spring, in various shades of blue-violet. Iris's two primary flower parts come in sets of three. First are three lower, spreading sepals, referred to as falls. Second are three upright petals called standards, which are pale to deep purple, with darker veins. Falls are wider than standards, and feature an intricately patterned spot with yellow highlights that serves as a nectary signal to bees, the plant's pollinator.

This native iris thrives in moist to wet conditions, so allow it to naturalize at the edge of wet areas. Here, it's not only beautiful, but helps control erosion, and provides cover and habitat for aquatic wildlife. Northern blue flag is ideal alongside and in ponds, rain gardens, creeks, and rivers, though it seems to do just as well in regular garden conditions.

Southern blue flag (*I. virginica*; 1-3 ft. × 1-3 ft.) is similar, but (as its name suggests) its geographic range doesn't extend as far north. The cultivars 'Gerald Darby' (2-3 ft. × 1½-2½ ft.) and 'Dark Aura' (2½-3 ft. × 1½-2 ft.) are selections of the hybrid *Iris ×robusta*, a cross of *I. versicolor* and *I. virginica*. Both of these cultivars feature spring foliage pigmented a dark violet color that fades later in the growing season, remaining only at the base of each leaf. Another cultivar to grow for foliage is 'Purple Flame', with dark purple leaves early in the season.

Iris versicolor makes a dependable, long-lived perennial addition to the deer-resistant native garden.

CULTURE AND TIPS

Northern blue flag grows in wet soils, even in water up to 4 in., and tolerates occasional flooding. It also does well where soil has plenty of moisture-retaining organic matter in lightly shaded or sunny beds and borders. Propagate in late summer, by dividing clumps of rhizomes, or scatter seed directly where you wish it to grow, covering lightly for winter dormancy. Once spring arrives and soil warms sufficiently, seed germinates readily and grows quickly. Snails may occasionally be a problem.

COMPANION PLANTS

Combine other moisture-loving plants with Northern blue flag. Blooming companions might include blue mistflower (*Conoclinium coelestinum*) and red cardinal flower (*Lobelia cardinalis*) in midsummer, which also complement blue flag's sword-like foliage. Red-osier dogwood (*Cornus sericea*), northern bayberry (*Morella pensylvanica*), and summersweet (*Clethra alnifolia*) provide a nice background.

DID YOU KNOW?

In many areas, especially wetlands, an invasive, fast-spreading European iris called yellow flag (*Iris pseudacorus*) often outcompetes and displaces many ecologically important native wetland plants, especially northern blue flag. Yellow flag is listed in the Global Invasive Species Database, and control of this invasive alien is necessary. It should never purposely be planted in wild areas or in the garden.

Liatris spicata DAISY FAMILY (ASTERACEAE)

Dense blazing star, spike gay feather

DEER RESISTANCE	HARDINESS ZONES	NORTHEAST NATIVE STATES	HEIGHT/SPREAD
8-10	3-8	CT, DC, DE, MA, MD, NJ, NY, PA, VA, WV	24-48 IN. × 9-18 IN.

Dense blazing star has upright, unbranched, leafy stems decorated with grassy foliage. The slender lower leaves may reach 5 in. long, and decrease in size farther up the stem. Stems are topped with a multitude of deep violet or white flower heads lacking true petals, which resemble bottlebrushes. The flower heads open from the top down, an anomaly in general and in the daisy family, where flowering sequence usually happens from the bottom up. Blazing star grows from underground corms planted just below the soil's surface in fall. Self-seeding is common.

Blazing star is highly prized in the cut flower industry, both fresh and dried. Popular cultivars include 'Floristan Violet' (36-48 in. × 12-18 in.) and 'Floristan White' (30-36 in. × 12-24 in.). 'Kobold' (18-30 in. × 6-12 in.) has stockier spikes of flowers. Smallhead blazing star (*L. micro-cephala*; 18-24 in. × 9-12 in.) is not as widely grown as its cousin, but it's just as gardenworthy. This plant also goes by the common names Appalachian blazing star and button snakeroot. Though its flower spikes are less robust than

dense blazing star, it is still useful at the front of perennial beds and borders, and in meadows and native plant gardens in particular. Flower stems bearing groups of three or four feathery, violet-purple flower heads bloom in July. Prairie blazing star (*L. pycnostachya*; 24-60 in. × 12-24 in.), an icon of those landscapes, has large, crowded flower spikes. It blooms midsummer for about a month.

CULTURE AND TIPS

In full sun or partly sunny spots, dense blazing star is easy to grow in average soil, especially those that are rich with compost or other organic material. It tolerates wetter soils than most species, as well as high temperatures and humidity. It can tolerate some drought once established, and accepts coastal conditions as well. Divide clumps of corms in early spring before growth commences, or in fall once top growth begins to fade. Seed-grown plants seldom bloom until their second season. Powdery mildew can be an issue where air circulation is poor.

Pink flowers of *Liatris spicata* make it a valuable summer perennial.

COMPANION PLANTS

Dense blazing star adds a wonderful verticality to the garden, and use of shorter plants that grow on a horizontal plane offers excellent contrast. Good candidates include purple cone-flower (*Echinacea purpurea*) and its numerous selections and cultivars; wine cups (*Callirhoe involucrata*); common sneezeweed (*Helenium autumnale*); and annual plains tickseed (*Coreopsis tinctoria*). Native grasses also work well, especially prairie dropseed (*Sporobolus heterolepis*), which thrives in similar conditions.

DID YOU KNOW?

The dried flowers of dense blazing star are vanilla-scented, and sometimes used in potpourri. Numerous species of butterflies are attracted by its nectar, and include monarchs, clouded sulphurs, painted ladies, and red admirals, to name a few. Bumblebees, digger bees, and leaf-cutting bees are frequent feeders, as are hummingbirds. Songbirds feast on seeds in fall.

93

Lobelia cardinalis BELLFLOWER FAMILY (CAMPANULACEAE)

Cardinal flower

DEER RESISTANCE	HARDINESS ZONES	NORTHEAST NATIVE STATES	HEIGHT/SPREAD
8-10	3-9	CT, DC, DE, MA, MD, ME, NH, NJ, NY, PA, RI, VA, VT, WV	2-4 FT. × 1-2 FT.

Lobelia siphilitica is a delightful color addition to the perennial garden in late summer.

Clump-forming cardinal flower is a short-lived perennial that overwinters by means of hardy rosettes, and often reseeds. Erect, unbranched stems are dressed in lance-shaped, toothed leaves, some 3 to 6 in. in length. Long spikes of two-lipped, tubular flowers in brilliant red (rarely pink or white) rise above the leafy basal rosettes. The upper lip is two-lobed, but the lower one is prominently three-lobed.

Cardinal flower is an excellent cut flower, and a staple of rain gardens and any other wet or poorly drained places in the garden. It provides bright impact in late summer for beds and borders.

Several selections, cultivars, and hybrids are on the market. 'Black Truffle' (3-4 ft. × 2-3 ft.) has foliage so darkly pigmented it is almost black, and this is paired with intense red flowers. 'Fried Green Tomatoes' (2-3 ft. × 2-2½ ft.) features paler, red-pigmented foliage, and excellent hardiness to boot. 'New Moon Maroon'

Red-flowered *Lobelia cardinalis* is one of the showiest deer-resistant native perennials.

[2-4 ft. × 1-2 ft.] shows off with deep maroon leaves that provide an outstanding contrast to bright red flowers. Great blue lobelia (*L. siphilitica*; 2-3 ft. × 1-1½ ft.) is similar, but with smaller blue flowers and a somewhat stockier habit. It is more perennial, and like its cousin, can be used to decorate damp places and rain gardens alike. In late summer, its leafy, blue racemes add vertical interest to plantings. Great blue lobelia is also found in a pure white form called 'Alba'.

CULTURE AND TIPS

Select a sunny or partly shaded spot in the garden where soil is high in organic matter and does not dry out in summer. Avoid covering the crowns with any mulch material. Deadhead spent flower spikes to encourage further bloom, and collect seed as it ripens if desired. Self-seeding is common. Slugs and snails can be a problem. The basal rosettes can be divided in spring, and will quickly establish and bloom the same summer.

COMPANION PLANTS

In rain gardens and other moist places, partner cardinal flower with swamp milkweed (*Asclepias incarnata*), especially its pure white-flowered cultivar 'Ice Ballet', blue mistflower

Cardinal flower is prized by hummingbirds.

(*Conoclinium coelestinum*), and earlier-blooming northern blue flag (*Iris versicolor*). The vertical flower spikes of dense blazing star (*Liatris spicata*) echo cardinal flower's habit. Sweetspire (*Itea virginica*) and winterberry (*Ilex verticillata*) make excellent background plantings, and also thrive in moist soil.

DID YOU KNOW?

Ruby-throated hummingbirds and spicebush swallowtail butterflies are the primary pollinators for cardinal flower. Its inclusion in residential gardens will almost always guarantee hummingbirds. Great blue lobelia attracts bumblebees and mason bees.

Monarda didyma MINT FAMILY (LAMIACEAE)

Scarlet beebalm, red bergamot

DEER RESISTANCE	HARDINESS ZONES	NORTHEAST NATIVE STATES	HEIGHT/SPREAD
7-9	4-9	CT, MA, MD, ME, NH, NJ, NY, PA, VA, VT, WV	2-4 FT. × 2-3 FT.

This robust, assertive perennial puts on a wonderful display of flowers for several weeks in summer. Its deep green, aromatic leaves are ovate and toothed, arranged in opposite pairs up square-shaped stems. Brilliant red, rounded, 3- to 4-in. clusters of arching, tubular flowers top the stems, perched above reddish purple bracts.

Extensive breeding has resulted in countless hybrids, reduced susceptibility to mildew, and smaller stature. The primary parents have been scarlet beebalm and light purple wild bergamot (*M. fistulosa*). 'Claire Grace' (3-4 ft. × 2-3 ft.) is a top-performing cultivar of the latter; 'Jacob Cline' (sometimes 'Kline' or 'Klein'; 3-5 ft. × 1½-2 ft.) may be the best cultivar of scarlet beebalm. Hybrids are now available with flowers in varying shades of pink, red, and purple, as well as white. The range of plant sizes has also expanded from about 1 ft. up to 4 ft. or more.

Resistance to powdery mildew varies considerably. Popular hybrids include hot pink *Monarda* 'Judith's Fancy Fuchsia' (3-4 ft. × 1½-2 ft.); brilliant red *M.* 'Gardenview Scarlet' (2-3 ft. × 1-2 ft.); and berry pink *M.* 'Raspberry Wine' (3-4 ft. × 2-3 ft.). Of the species, eastern beebalm (*M. bradburiana*; 1-2 ft. × 1-2 ft.) may be the most mildew resistant. In late spring, it displays masses of pale pink flowers spotted with purple on the lip. Long-blooming spotted beebalm or horsemint (*M. punctata*; 1-2 ft. × 9 in.-1 ft.) is also notable, with good resistance to mildew. Instead of terminal clusters of flowers, here the clusters are stacked up the stem, subtended by colorful, leaf-like bracts in pink or white. The true flowers are hooded, yellow, and copiously spotted with brownish purple, magnets for pollinating insects, especially beneficial wasps.

All beebalms are ideal for planting in meadows, native, pollinator, and wildlife gardens, as well as in cutting, edible flower, and herb gardens. Mingle them with shrubs in informal mixed beds and borders. Shorter selections grow well in containers.

CULTURE AND TIPS

Scarlet beebalm grows as well in full sun as part shade, especially where summers are hot. Rich, well-drained soil, amended with moisture-retentive compost or other organic matter, is ideal. Soil must remain moist, as scarlet beebalm is susceptible to powdery mildew that attacks when plants are stressed and air movement is poor. Overcrowded plants can be pruned to thin stems, or thinned by division. Divide by lifting the rhizomes in spring or fall every three to four years, or as needed, to control their spread and renew vigor. Sow seeds directly after frost. Beebalms are rabbit and deer resistant, and tolerate planting near black walnut trees.

COMPANION PLANTS

Scarlet beebalm combines well with many other perennials, particularly dense blazing star (*Liatris spicata*), black-eyed Susan (*Rudbeckia hirta*), and prairie rosinweed (*Silphium terebinthinaceum*). Little bluestem (*Schizachyrium scoparium*) and prairie dropseed (*Sporobolus heterolepis*) provide grassy cover for the plant's fading lower leaves toward the end of summer.

DID YOU KNOW?

The name beebalm comes from its use as a remedy for bee stings. Native Americans of the Iroquois tribe who inhabited what became the town of Oswego, New York used the leaves for tea, as did colonial Americans after the Boston tea party. Add the edible flowers to fruit salads and jellies. In addition to bees—especially bumblebees—a large variety of butterflies, beetles, and wasps visit beebalm, as well as ruby-throated hummingbirds. Songbirds harvest the seed in winter. Crush and rub the aromatic leaves on skin to help repel mosquitos.

Monarda didyma is a favorite of hummingbirds and butterflies.

Penstemon digitalis SNAPDRAGON FAMILY (SCROPHULARIACEAE)

Foxglove beardtongue, smooth beardtongue

DEER RESISTANCE	HARDINESS ZONES	NORTHEAST NATIVE STATES	HEIGHT/SPREAD
9-10	3-8	CT, DC, DE, MA, MD, ME, NH, NJ, NY, PA, RI, VA, VT, WV	36-60 IN. × 18-24 IN.

This clumping native blooms from mid- to late spring with clusters of white, two-lipped, tubular flowers on the tips of upright stems. The upper lip is two-lobed, the lower three-lobed; there are five stamens, only four of which are fertile. Blooms are followed by reddish seedpods that split open when ripe to disseminate seed. Basal leaves of foxglove beardtongue turn attractive shades of reddish to bronze in the cooling temperatures of fall, and provide winter interest as a handsome ground cover.

Hairy beardtongue (*P. hirsutus*; 18-20 in. × 10-12 in.), with its fuzzy-stemmed, lavender-purple flowers, is similar to those of the above, but blooms somewhat earlier. Eastern smooth beardtongue (*P. laevigatus*; 12-36 in. × 12-18 in.) is relatively rare, and has pale purple to white flowers on hairless stems from late spring into midsummer. Small's penstemon (*P. smallii*; 18-30 in. × 18-24 in.) presents its panicles of tubular, pink or lavender flowers from late spring to early summer.

Allow beardtongue to naturalize in native plant and wildflower gardens, as well as meadows, cottage gardens, and rock gardens. This plant fits well into formal residential gardens too, and is an excellent source of cut flowers.

CULTURE AND TIPS

Foxglove beardtongue does best in soils that drain well. In the wild, it will inhabit moist areas as long as the soil is well drained, and it receives full sun. Average, loamy soil is fine, and it tolerates clay soils, preferably in full sun, but part shade is best in hot summer regions. Once established, it is moderately drought tolerant. Direct sow seed as soon as it ripens in early fall; it will germinate the following spring. Remove spent flower spikes if self-seeding is not desired. Otherwise, divide the crowns of multiple plants

Penstemon digitalis is found in the wild in white, although several cultivars offer variety in flower and foliage color.

into singles in spring or fall, depending upon your climate. Pests and diseases are few, but root rot may occur in overly wet conditions, especially in winter.

COMPANION PLANTS

Effective companions for foxglove beardtongue are blue star (*Amsonia tabernaemontana*) and dense blazing star (*Liatris spicata*). It looks lovely backed by Virginia sweetspire (*Itea virginica*) and arrowwood viburnum (*Viburnum dentatum*). The mounding, fine leaves of prairie dropseed (*Sporobolus heterolepis*) provide good foliage contrast.

DID YOU KNOW?

This plant's sterile stamen (or staminode) is tufted with bristly hairs like a beard, hence the common name beardtongue. Perhaps coincidentally, long-tongued bees are the primary pollinators of beardtongue—indeed, eight different species visit, including mason bees, leafcutter bees, sweat bees, and bumblebees. Beneficial wasps also harvest pollen. Syrphid flies forage for pollen, but are seldom efficient pollinators. Butterflies and hummingbirds drink the nectar, and the seed provides food for songbirds.

Polemonium reptans PHLOX FAMILY (POLEMONIACEAE)
Jacob's ladder, Greek valerian

DEER RESISTANCE	HARDINESS ZONES	NORTHEAST NATIVE STATES	HEIGHT/SPREAD
7-9	3-8	CT, DC, DE, MA, MD, NH, NJ, NY, PA, RI, VA, VT, WV	12-18 IN. × 12-18 IN.

This native is an ideal groundcover for woodlands and cool, shaded locations. The alternate, compound leaves, which grow close to the ground, reach about 8 in. in length, and are composed of pairs of 1 in.-long, oval leaflets arranged on stems like rungs on a ladder. Loose, pendant clusters of open, bell-shaped flowers appear the second half of spring. These are pale to dark blue, each about ¾ in., and terminate the soft, sprawling stems. Dry, tan-colored fruits follow, and split to release seeds when they are ripe.

Jacob's ladder is ideal in lightly or partially shaded, naturalized native plant gardens, woodlands, and pollinator gardens, as well as in informal beds and borders.

Several cultivars are on the market, including white-flowered 'Alba' and bright 'Blue Pearl'. Blue-flowered 'Stairway to Heaven' has leaflets rimmed in creamy white, as does pink-budded 'Touch of Class'. Also variegated, 'Brize D'Anjou' is sometimes considered a cultivar of *P. reptans*, but, correctly, it belongs to European species *P. caeruleum*.

CULTURE AND TIPS

Low maintenance Jacob's ladder thrives in partly shaded spots where the soil is high in humus and drains well, but does not dry out in summer. In cool climates, this plant tolerates full sun. Under good growing conditions, plants will seed about copiously, and some gardeners find it aggressive. If needed, deadhead spent flower stems to the base in late spring to extend the bloom season, reduce self-seeding, and encourage a second flush of bloom. Later in summer, when the leaves look rough, this plant responds well to being trimmed to the ground, and will regrow with fresh, green foliage. Transplant seedlings in mid-spring, or sow seed directly in fall for germination the following spring. Plants may also be divided, and soft stem cuttings root readily in spring. Jacob's ladder also tolerates soil conditions beneath black walnut trees, where many other plants do not.

The clear blue flowers of *Polemonium reptans* make for a cheery spring display.

COMPANION PLANTS

Consider partnering early meadow rue (*Thalictrum dioicum*) with Jacob's ladder, especially under trees in light woodlands. Celandine poppy (*Stylophorum diphyllum*) is another appropriate companion. Ferns, including lady fern (*Athyrium filix-femina*) and marginal wood fern (*Dryopteris marginalis*), make an excellent backdrop to show off this plant's lovely blue flowers. After bloom time, the grassy foliage of seersucker sedge (*Carex plantaginea*) provides textural contrast to its attractive, ladder-like foliage, which remains through most of summer.

DID YOU KNOW?

Many pollinators are hard put to find food available early in the season, and are drawn to Jacob's ladder for both nectar and pollen. Large bees like bumblebees, mason bees, and small carpenter bees are among the most frequent visitors. Its nectar attracts moths and butterflies. Folklore tells of its use historically for various complaints, from snakebites to heart palpitations, hysteria, and epilepsy. An herbal tea made from the root is said to relieve coughs and congestion from colds.

Pycnanthemum muticum MINT FAMILY (LAMIACEAE)

Mountain mint, clustered mountain mint

DEER RESISTANCE	HARDINESS ZONES	NORTHEAST NATIVE STATES	HEIGHT/SPREAD
9-10	4-8	CT, DC, DE, MA, MD, ME, NH, NJ, NY, PA, RI, VA, VT, WV	24-36 IN. × 24-36 IN.

Mountain mint is one of the most beneficial plants for pollinators. Although the flowers are not considered showy, their nectar certainly attracts bees, butterflies, flies, wasps, and hummingbirds, with months of appeal. The plant is also the preferred host for several butterfly caterpillars. A clumping perennial with aromatic foliage, mountain mint naturalizes readily, and because it can spread quickly by rhizomes, can be an aggressive perennial in the garden. Typical of the mint family, mountain mint has erect, square, branched stems clothed with opposite pairs of aromatic, pointed, oval- to lance-shaped leaves, which are rimmed with teeth. Terminal groups of small, pinkish, tubular flowers bloom from midsummer to fall. Individual flowers are two-lipped, and collected into flat-topped, crowded clusters above conspicuous, showy bracts, silver with long hairs.

Other species of mountain mint with varying native ranges are available, and similar in size, appearance, and habit. These include narrow-leaved or slender mountain mint (*P. tenuifolium*), hoary mountain mint (*P. incanum*), and Virginia or American mountain mint

(*P. virginianum*). All have aromatic foliage and flowers arranged in clusters. Not unexpectedly, narrow-leaf mountain mint has very slender leaves and larger clusters of white flowers. Hoary mountain mint has lavender-tinged flowers, purple-spotted on the lower lip, arranged in tiers up the stem, and subtended by silver-dusted bracts; leaves are also dredged with silver, both above and below. The narrow, entire leaves of white-flowered Virginia mountain mint taper to a point, and are glossy. All species are superb in wildlife, pollinator, and native plant gardens, as well as in herb gardens, cottage, and cut flower gardens (for both fresh and dry cuts), and massed in open areas. Plant near vegetable gardens to attract pollinating bees.

CULTURE AND TIPS

Vigorous, easy-to-grow mountain mint thrives in full sun to light shade in average soils that drain well. Although somewhat drought tolerant, this species does not enjoy dry roots, and these conditions will curb its aggressiveness. If overly assertive, remove unwanted spreading rhizomes back to the crown. Be aware that beds with

Pycnanthemum muticum has leaves that emit a strong minty scent when crushed.

moist, rich soil and thick mulch provide perfect conditions for this plant's aggressive tendencies—poor, dry soils can be an asset in keeping it in check. Pests and diseases are few. Allow plants to remain standing into fall and beyond to provide fragrant, vertical winter interest. Sow seeds directly on the surface of the seedbed in fall to germinate the following spring. Otherwise, increase by division in late summer. Mountain mint makes an outstanding and long-lasting cut flower addition to summer bouquets.

COMPANION PLANTS

Mountain mint makes bold masses and benefits aesthetically from less dense companions. Try prairie rosinweed (*Silphium terebinthinaceum*) to add background height to a planting. Prairie blazing star (*Liatris pycnostachya*) adds verticality. Consider wine cups (*Callirhoe involucrata*) as

a groundcover at the base of mountain mint for a different texture, and annual brown-eyed Susan (*Rudbeckia triloba*) to add a dash of bright color. The butterfly-attracting spikes of fragrant white summersweet (*Clethra alnifolia*) provide a good backdrop, especially in damp soils.

DID YOU KNOW?

Crush leaves of mountain mint and rub on the skin to deter mosquitoes. A great many butterfly species are attracted to this plant: eastern short-tailed blues, fritillaries, Northern broken dash, olive and other hairstreaks are just a sampling of the visitors seeking nectar. The plant also entertains beneficial ladybugs and lacewing bugs, among others. Moths, hummingbirds, and countless species of bees absolutely adore mountain mint, and it's amazing the delightful and literal buzz this plant creates.

Rudbeckia fulgida DAISY FAMILY (ASTERACEAE)

Orange coneflower, perennial black-eyed Susan

DEER RESISTANCE	HARDINESS ZONES	NORTHEAST NATIVE STATES	HEIGHT/SPREAD
9-10	3-9	CT, DC, DE, MA, MD, NJ, NY, PA, VA, WV	12-36 IN. × 24-30 IN.

Long-blooming from midsummer to fall, orange coneflower varies across its native range. Generally, the stems and foliage are covered with bristly hairs, making for a rather coarse effect. Its 2- to 3-in. wide, daisy-like flower heads are golden yellow, centered with a purplish brown disk, and each ray petal is toothed at the tip. The plant spreads by rhizomes and develops into sizable colonies over time.

Nomenclature for orange coneflower is confused at best. The best-known cultivar may be 'Goldsturm'. When it was introduced, it became one of the most popular garden plants, and was named perennial plant of the year by the Perennial Plant Association in 1999. No wonder—its qualifications include bushy but uniform, mounded habit; profuse, strikingly large blooms; long flowering season; attractiveness to butterflies and other pollinators;

its role as a late-season seed source to birds; and general good manners. *Rudbeckia* 'American Gold Rush' is a naturally compact cultivar with outstandingly bright yellow-gold flowers from July to September and high resistance to fungal *Septoria* leaf spot. It was selected as a 2020 award winner among herbaceous perennials by All-America Selections, a nonprofit organization that trials plants.

Rough, hairy black-eyed Susan (*R. hirta*), the state flower of Maryland, has naturalized happily throughout much of North America. Its gloriously cheerful, dark-eyed, orange to gold daisies are widely recognized from early summer well into fall. Though a short-lived perennial, it seeds about freely, tolerates all but the most extreme growing conditions, and is parent to numerous cultivars. Semi- or fully double orange and rust 'Gloriosa' (or 'Gloriosa Double Flowered')

Rudbeckia fulgida is a mainstay of the summer garden, and mixes well with other sun-loving native plants.

was an All-America Selections winner in 1981. 'Sonora' has 5-in. golden flowers with a very large, chocolate-colored eye, a breakthrough in color breeding. 'Cherry Brandy' is unusual for its black-eyed cherry-colored blooms. The hybrid strain 'Autumn Colors' has large, bicolored daisies that range from yellow and gold through orange and reddish bronze; 'Cherokee Sunset' strain is similarly colored, but with slightly shorter stems. Mid-sized 'Chim Chiminee' strain has slender or quilled flowers in yellow, gold, orange, or mahogany.

Cutleaf or tall coneflower (*R. laciniata*) may reach 9 ft. tall. Its long stems are clothed with deeply divided, jagged-edged leaves, and terminate in clusters of sparsely rayed flower heads, each with a green, rounded central cone. The variety *hortensia*, an heirloom plant sometimes known as 'Golden Glow', is fully double-flowered with abundant, almost fluffy flower heads of brilliant yellow. It's also commonly known as "outhouse plant," a reference to its longtime use around outhouses. Double-flowered 'Goldquelle' (or 'Gold Fountain') spreads much more slowly, and seldom tops 3 ft. 'Autumn Sun' (or 'Herbstsonne') is a notable giant hybrid with huge, green-eyed flower heads on stems that may reach 7 to 8 ft.

Flower heads of great coneflower (*R. maxima*) rise from a basal rosette of blue-green foliage to 8 ft. or more. Its flowers have drooping, golden ray petals and tall, dark, pointed cones, 2 to 5 in. in height.

All these are superb plants for meadow and native wildflower plantings. Dress up the back of sunny cottage garden beds and borders with some of the taller species; select mid-sized species for use in more formal areas, and with shrubs in foundation plantings. Orange coneflowers are tough and resilient plants, making them perfect for urban gardens.

CULTURE AND TIPS

Plant orange coneflower in full or part sun for best results. It thrives in fertile, well-draining soil; amend with organic matter to improve structure and maintain even moisture if need be. Deadhead routinely to extend bloom time and interrupt self-seeding. Be on the lookout for powdery mildew, the result of humid summer weather. This may affect the plant's aesthetics, but won't affect its performance.

COMPANION PLANTS

There are plenty of companion species that complement orange coneflower. Appealing companions that succeed in similar growing conditions include wild bergamot (*Monarda fistulosa*), wild petunia (*Ruellia humilis*), and rattlesnake master (*Eryngium yuccifolium*). As far as foliage companions, consider little bluestem grass (*Schizachyrium scoparium*) and tufted hair grass (*Deschampsia cespitosa*).

DID YOU KNOW?

The primary pollinators for orange coneflower are bees looking for both pollen and nectar. It is a host plant for caterpillars of silvery checkerspot butterflies, and several other butterfly species visit for nectar during bloom time. After flowering, the remaining seedheads are particularly attractive to seed-eating songbirds, especially goldfinches.

Ruellia caroliniensis ACANTHUS FAMILY (ACANTHACEAE)

Carolina wild petunia, hairy wild petunia

DEER RESISTANCE	HARDINESS ZONES	NORTHEAST NATIVE STATES	HEIGHT/SPREAD
9-10	6-10	DC, DE, MD, NJ, PA, VA, WV	24-36 IN. × 15-18 IN.

From late spring well into summer, clumps of Carolina wild petunia bloom almost continuously in lavender to white, each flower for only a single day. Its 1-in., hairy, tubular flowers are slender, with five-pointed lobes traced with deep purple at the throat. These typically occur in axial and terminal clusters, but may be solitary. Unbranched stems and olive green, oblong leaves are covered with hairs. This species tends to spread by means of reseeding. Seed capsules discharge their bounty explosively at times, up to several feet away from the parent plant, and seedlings should be monitored to avoid over-crowding within the garden. This plant is perfect for rock gardens, path edges, and as a long-flowering selection at the base of other much taller plants, especially viewed from a pathway.

Carolina wild petunia also has a white form that comes true from seed. Related *Ruellia*

humilis (1½-2 ft. × 1½-2 ft.), with tubular flowers in lavender-purple, is also commonly called wild petunia. It's a very similar plant, but more upright, and thrives in dryish, loose soils in full sun. This species can be a very aggressive reseeder under certain conditions, quickly overtaking unplanted garden areas, especially gravel pathways and open, sunny spots.

CULTURE AND TIPS

Carolina wild petunia adapts to various cultural conditions from part sun to light shade. It tolerates the dappled shade of deciduous trees. Sandy or average soil that drains freely is best; it prefers for the soil to remain damp during the heat of summer, but will tolerate some drought. Sow seed directly in fall as it ripens, or store refrigerated until spring and direct sow then. If collecting your own seed, carefully observe the ripening capsules as they change from

The white form of *Ruellia caroliniensis* blooms profusely in the author's garden.

green to brown, and collect prior to when they split and expose the seeds (usually about 2 months after bloom). Allow this plant to naturalize in rock gardens, or use it as a ground cover along paths and bed edges. Excellent in pollinator and native plant gardens, especially where soils are poor and dry.

COMPANION PLANTS

Combine with mountain mint (*Pycnanthemum muticum*), wine cups (*Callirhoe involucrata*), and spotted beebalm (*Monarda punctata*) in native plant gardens. Suitable companion grasses include prairie dropseed (*Sporobolus heterolepis*) and tufted hair grass (*Deschampsia cespitosa*).

DID YOU KNOW?

Butterflies and bees are frequent visitors to Carolina wild petunia for its abundant nectar. It is the larval host plant for caterpillars of common buckeye, white peacock, and fatima butterflies.

Salvia lyrata MINT FAMILY (LAMIACEAE)

Lyre-leaf sage, cancer weed

DEER RESISTANCE	HARDINESS ZONES	NORTHEAST NATIVE STATES	HEIGHT/SPREAD
8-10	5-8	CT, DC, DE, MD, NJ, NY, PA, VA, WV	1-2 FT. × ¾-1 FT.

'Purple Volcano' is a seed strain cultivar of lyre-leaf sage featuring reddish foliage and white flowers.

Lyre-leaf sage blooms from mid- to late spring with slender, erect, square stems clothed with sparse flower spikes. These display showy whorls of two-lipped, tubular, lavender flowers, each about 1 in. long. The two-lobed lower lip and three-lobed upper lip form a hood. Its leaves are lobed unevenly, veined with purple, and arranged in compact basal rosettes; in winter these often turn purplish. This sage self-seeds and naturalizes extensively, so deadheading is essential.

'Purple Knockout' [1½-2 ft. × 1-1½ ft.] is a good cultivar, with shiny, deep purple leaves that often lighten in summer. 'Purple Volcano' [½-¾ ft. × ¾-1 ft.] is said to retain its foliage color more effectively through summer sun. Both cultivars seed around freely, come true from seed, and tolerate summer heat and drought. They are valuable semi-evergreen groundcovers, perhaps to replace common, non-native bugleweed (*Ajuga reptans*) in gardens. Lyre-leaf sage is an interesting early-blooming addition to rock gardens and cottage gardens, as well as in wildflower and even rooftop gardens.

Clumping azure blue sage (*S. azurea*; 3–5 ft. × 1½–2 ft.) is a large cousin that also prefers full sun, and it tolerates drought as well as heat and humidity. Its slender foliage is grayish green, and its heavenly blue, two-lipped flowers are arranged in whorls on terminal spikes. Cut stems by half in late spring to encourage more compact and sturdy growth. The variety *grandiflora* has larger flowers than the species. 'Nekan' is a seed strain from the Nebraska-Kansas border area that has larger flowers and a more robust, compact habit.

Scarlet sage (*S. coccinea*; 2–3 ft. × ¾–1 ft.) is frequently grown as an annual in northern regions. In the wild, it grows as an upright sub-shrub. Stems carry opposite pairs of triangular hairy leaves, each scalloped along the rim. Whorls of brilliant red, two-lipped flowers are widely spaced in long, upright terminal clusters. 'Coral Nymph' (1–1½ ft. × ¾–1 ft.) has lovely coral pink flowers; 'Lady in Red' (2–3 ft. × 1½–2 ft.) speaks for itself.

Tolerant both of heat and humidity, autumn sage (*S. greggii*; 1–4 ft. × 2–3 ft.) is evergreen and becomes woody at the base in mild climates; elsewhere it is treated as an annual. It is very long-blooming, with terminal clusters of ¼- to 1-in., two-lipped flowers arranged in pairs along hairy stems. These come in white, red, pink, yellow, or violet. Cut this species back after the first flush of bloom to encourage rebloom. Available cultivars include 'Wild Thing' (2–3 ft. × 2–3 ft.) with abundant coral pink flowers; scarlet red-flowered 'Maraschino' (3–4 ft. × 2–3 ft.); apricot 'California Sunset' (1½–3 ft. × 3–4 ft.); blushing white 'Teresa' (1–2 ft. × 1–2 ft.); and pink-purple 'Diane' (1–1½ ft. × 3–4 ft.).

CULTURE AND TIPS

Lyre-leaf sage does best in full sun, although a touch of shade is acceptable. It thrives in a wide range of well-drained soils, but can often be found in wet or damp places in the wild. Deadhead for a second flush of bloom, and to avoid excessive self-seeding. Direct sow seed or divide established plants in spring or fall.

COMPANION PLANTS

Sage makes an outstanding companion to so many other natives as long as soil drainage is good. Partner with smallhead blazing star (*Liatris microcephala*), sneezeweed (*Helenium autumnale*), and Indian pink (*Spigelia marilandica*). Try lyre-leaf sage as a groundcover at the base of New Jersey tea (*Ceanothus americanus*), American beautyberry (*Callicarpa americana*), and shrubby St. John's wort (*Hypericum prolificum*).

DID YOU KNOW?

At one time a poultice was made from the leaves of lyre-leaf sage as a remedy for skin cancer and warts. The roots were made into a salve to soothe sores. Nectar-seeking bees are frequent visitors to the flowers; when they

Salvia lyrata flowers with lavender spikes in spring.

land on the lower lip of each flower, their weight causes the stamens to tip and brush pollen onto the bees' backs. Hummingbirds and butterflies also visit the flowers to harvest nectar. The seed supplies food for songbirds.

Senna marilandica PEA FAMILY (FABACEAE)

Maryland senna

DEER RESISTANCE	HARDINESS ZONES	NORTHEAST NATIVE STATES	HEIGHT/SPREAD
9-10	4-9	DC, DE, MD, PA, VA, WV	36-72 IN. × 24-36 IN.

Maryland senna is an important nectar and pollen source for native bumblebees and other pollinators.

Also known as *Cassia marilandica*, Maryland senna blooms from mid- to late summer with showy, brilliant yellow flowers that congregate in long clusters in leaf axils, as well as at stem tips. Each five-parted pea-like blossom has ten dark brown stamens; the lower four have long filaments and long anthers, while the middle three have short filaments and long anthers, and the upper three are short on both counts, and sterile. The prominent style curves upwards to receive pollen. The stems carry alternate, six- to eight-paired, pinnate leaves on short leaf stalks. Seedpods ripen much later after flowering, provide interest through fall, and remain on the plant well into winter.

Magnificent and imposing, this plant's tall, unbranched stems are sturdy, and handle winds with aplomb thanks to its wide-spreading, stabilizing root system. Perfect for butterfly gardens, rain gardens, along the edge of woodlands, and

Senna marilandica brightens the summer garden, and thrives in even the poorest soils.

at the back of cottage gardens to add height. Maryland senna is also appropriate at the back of beds and borders, in native plant and pollinator gardens, and even as an informal perennial hedge along fences or property lines.

CULTURE AND TIPS

Maryland senna is found in the wild in damp places, but it adapts well to well-drained clay or sandy soils, and is tolerant of occasional flooding. It does well in full sun as well as part shade, and endures summer heat and humidity. Pests and diseases are few. Dried foliage is aromatic, resulting in resistance to rabbits as well as deer. Start from seed, but nick the seed first and soak overnight for more efficient germination. Plants do not divide well, so site accordingly in an appropriate location.

COMPANION PLANTS

Moisture-loving plants are especially valuable as companions for Maryland senna. Consider planting annual, yellow-flowered partridge pea (*Chamaechrista fasciculata*) as a color echo. Swamp milkweed (*Asclepias incarnata*) and New York ironweed (*Vernonia novaboracensis*) are compatible also, along with late spring-blooming northern blue flag (*Iris versicolor*) to extend the season and offer a foliage contrast. Due to its considerable stature, Maryland senna works well with native shrubs such as winterberry (*Ilex verticillata*) and northern bayberry (*Morella pensylvanica*).

DID YOU KNOW?

Senna tea has been a traditional herbal remedy for constipation for generations. The plant is an important larval host for many butterfly species such as cloudless sulphurs, orange-barred sulphurs, and sleepy oranges. The fallen seed of Maryland senna are a food source for wild turkeys in fall.

Silphium terebinthinaceum DAISY FAMILY (ASTERACEAE)
Prairie rosinweed, prairie dock

DEER RESISTANCE	HARDINESS ZONES	NORTHEAST NATIVE STATES	HEIGHT/SPREAD
8-10	4-8	DC, VA, WV	3-10 FT. × 1-3 FT.

Prairie rosinweed has bright yellow flowers that seem to glow on tall stems in summer.

Prairie rosinweed is no shrinking violet, with basal clumps of oval or heart-shaped leaves, to 18 in. or more, that grow from its taproot. Leaf undersides are rough, as if covered with sandpaper—too coarse even for rabbits. Flower heads with bright yellow ray petals are carried on green stems (sometimes slightly purplish red) that are more or less leafless, and branch toward the top. They appear from midsummer to early fall.

Mohr's rosinweed (*S. mohrii*; 2-5 ft. × 2-3 ft.) is not as well known, but its smaller stature may be appropriate for gardens where space is limited. Its architectural presence is undeniable; copious clusters of pale yellow, 2-in. flowers bloom well into fall atop its hairy, branched stems. Also underused is similar Simpson's rosinweed (*S. simpsonii*; 4-5 ft. × 2-3 ft.), with 2- to 3-in. flowers that provide food for bees and

117

Silphium terebinthinaceum features large, pubescent leaves that deer avoid.

butterflies late in the season. More widely cultivated is compass plant (*S. laciniatum*; 5–9 ft. × 1½–3 ft.), with huge basal leaves cut almost to the midrib. These leaves are usually oriented on a north-south axis (hence the plant's common name) so as to avoid intense prairie sun and maximize water use. Widely spaced, 5-in., sunflower-like blooms of yellow alternate on the upper stems. Rhizomatous cup plant (*S. perfoliatum*; 4–8 ft. × 1–3 ft.) is vigorous to borderline aggressive, and bears pairs of clasping leaves up the stem. The unique structure of these leaves allows rainwater to collect and creates small pools where songbirds often drink—it also deters insects from climbing to feed on the yellow flower heads.

Silphium is magnificent planted in large meadows, wildflower, native plant, and cutting gardens, and provides vertical accent to the back of deep beds and borders. All plants in the genus exude a rosin-like sap when wounded, thus the common name rosinweed. This same sap makes them unpalatable to deer and other mammals.

CULTURE AND TIPS

Prairie rosinweed is easy to grow in full sun and average soils that are well drained. These plants tolerate clay well, and some recognize them as "clay busters." Their exceptionally deep taproots make them very drought tolerant, but once established, moving plants successfully is virtually impossible. In spite of their towering height, staking is seldom necessary due to their strong, fibrous stems. Start seed outdoors in fall for germination the following spring.

COMPANION PLANTS

Rosinweeds are signature plants of the prairies, so they combine well with other meadow plants. Attractive candidates include pale purple coneflower (*Echinacea pallida*), wild bergamot (*Monarda fistulosa*), and prairie blazing star (*Liatris pycnostachya*). Suggested grass companions are pink muhly grass (*Muhlenbergia capillaris*) and switchgrass (*Panicum virgatum*).

DID YOU KNOW?

In earlier times, the sticky rosin produced by *Silphium* species was used as a type of chewing gum. Bumblebees and honeybees visit to harvest nectar, as do ruby-throated hummingbirds. The plant's copious seed provides food for goldfinches and other seed-eating birds, which in turn play an important role in seed distribution.

Spigelia marilandica LOGAN FAMILY [LOGANIACEAE]
Indian pink, pinkroot

DEER RESISTANCE:	HARDINESS ZONES:	NORTHEAST NATIVE STATES:	HEIGHT/SPREAD:
8-10	5-9	MD, VA	12-24 IN. × 12-16 IN.

This long-lived clumping perennial is an exquisite addition to gardens when it blooms in late spring to early summer. Its scarlet, tubular flowers, canary yellow within, gather in one-sided clusters atop erect, unbranched stems that are clothed in pairs of deep green, oval leaves. It self-seeds by explosively splitting and discharging (termed dehiscing) seed capsules, which makes a noticeable popping sound. The upright trumpet flowers present an invitation to passing hummingbirds to drink their nectar.

'Little Redhead' [1½-2 ft. × 1¾-2 ft.] is a compact cultivar. Indian pink is attractive in hummingbird gardens, woodland gardens in high shade, cottage gardens, rain gardens, and cut flower gardens.

CULTURE AND TIPS

Indian pink thrives in average well-drained soil amended with moisture-retaining compost or other organic matter prior to planting. It prefers bright shade, but is found in the wild in both sunny and shaded spots. Propagation is best by dividing mature clumps in spring shortly after growth begins. Be mindful of disturbing the fleshy roots as little as possible. Keep consistently watered until it is well established. If deadheaded right after blooms fade, a second crop of flowers will often appear.

COMPANION PLANTS

Many native woodland plants mix well with Indian pink. Consider intermediate wood fern

Spigelia marilandica adds a riot of red and yellow to the early summer garden.

(*Dryopteris intermedia*), red columbine (*Aquilegia canadensis*), and green-and-gold (*Chrysogonum virginianum*) as companions, especially in bright woodlands. Two native shrubs that make useful companions are arrowwood viburnum (*Viburnum dentatum*) and spicebush (*Lindera benzoin*). There are also three sedges that work well: seersucker sedge (*Carex plantaginea*), broadleaf sedge (*Carex platyphylla*), and Appalachian sedge (*Carex appalachica*).

DID YOU KNOW?

Once established in the garden, Indian pink is a long-lived and dependable native, free from diseases and pests. It is well worth the effort to find the correct spot for it—in flower, a mature plant is a most stunning sight to behold. It's a favorite of ruby-throated hummingbirds and butterflies.

121

Stylophorum diphyllum POPPY FAMILY (PAPAVERACEAE)
Celandine poppy

DEER RESISTANCE	HARDINESS ZONES	NORTHEAST NATIVE STATES	HEIGHT/SPREAD
8-10	4-9	DC, DE, MD, PA, VA, WV	12-18 IN. × 8-12 IN.

In mid-spring, this woodland poppy promises clusters of colorful bright yellow, 1- to 2-in. flowers. Thick, rhizomatous roots produce rosettes of pubescent, deep green, cut and lobed leaves, to 6-in. long. The leaf and flower stems are also hairy. Nodding buds, each enclosed in a pair of bristly sepals, congregate in clusters atop stems. Each four-petaled flower is bright yellow, centered with a boss (or large cluster) of numerous stamens. These are mostly pollinated by bees and other beneficial insects, but also self-pollinate. Fertilized flowers develop into dangling, oval, four-chambered seed capsules that split open to release black seeds in mid- to late summer.

Celandine poppy is suitable for shaded beds and borders, as well as more naturalistic areas in the garden. It excels as much in moderate to deep shade as on woodland edges.

CULTURE AND TIPS

In the wild, celandine poppy thrives in damp, shaded woodlands where soil is high in organic matter, and providing similar growing conditions in the garden in full to part shade proves effective. If soil dries out in summer, plants will benefit from an application of an organic mulch. In optimal conditions, this poppy seeds about freely, and some gardeners consider it aggressive, yet it's easily kept in check. Propagate from seed sown directly in winter, and thin after germination. Be alert for damage from slugs and snails—fortunately, rabbits, as well as deer, find this plant unpalatable.

COMPANION PLANTS

Celandine poppy combines beautifully with many other spring-blooming natives. Consider the early-to-bloom red columbine (*Aquilegia*

Most poppies prefer sun, but *Stylophorum diphyllum* brightens woodlands.

canadensis], with its cultivars such as dwarf 'Little Lanterns' and all-yellow 'Corbett', as well as later-blooming Indian pink (*Spigelia marilandica*), with its trumpet-shaped flowers of yellow and scarlet. Wild bleeding heart (*Dicentra eximia*) and annual harlequin corydalis (*Capnoides sempervirens*) make fine companions too. Use of the groundcover green-and-gold (*Chrysogonum virginianum*) creates a darker yellow color echo for the poppies. Evergreen Christmas fern (*Polystichum acrostichoides*) and durable marginal wood fern (*Dryopteris marginalis*) also make excellent companions.

DID YOU KNOW?

The bright orange sap of celandine poppy is acrid and caustic on the skin, but it has been used fresh to treat corns and warts. In Russia, it is used purportedly against cancer, and has been employed by European herbalists for numerous complaints over the centuries. Native Americans used the sap as a yellow dye. Mice feed on the seeds, and help to distribute them. Don't mistake this native for greater celandine (*Cheliodonium majus*), a poppy relative and highly invasive European plant with smaller, less attractive flowers.

Thalictrum dioicum BUTTERCUP FAMILY (RANUNCULACEAE)

Early meadow rue, quicksilver weed

DEER RESISTANCE:	HARDINESS ZONES:	NORTHEAST NATIVE STATES:	HEIGHT/SPREAD:
9-10	3-7	CT, DC, DE, MA, MD, ME, NH, NJ, NY, PA, RI, VA, VT, WV	12-24 IN. × 12-24 IN.

In spring, early meadow rue blooms profusely, its petal-less flowers a pale off-white. These feathery flowers appear by the hundreds on each plant, and close inspection reveals they differ from plant to plant. This is because early meadow rue is dioecious, meaning it has male and female flowers on separate plants. All lack petals, and the numerous visible flower parts are either stamens (male) or pistils (female). The 1/4-in. flowers of both sexes cluster in loose, branching panicles on the upper parts of purple-tinged stems. Male flowers bud with short-lived white sepals that drop; they then open to flaunt clumps of dangling, tassel-like, cream-colored stamens. Female flowers show only their ten, greenish white, spidery pistils. Pollination is achieved by wind, and if successful, ridged green fruits called achenes develop by early summer. Finely textured, grayish green foliage is much like that of columbine. Sometimes curious fawns sample the young foliage, but damage is seldom more than a nibble.

Purple meadow rue (*T. dasycarpum*; 3-7 ft. × 3-4 ft.) is similar but much taller, prefers full sun, and blooms in early summer. The 3/8-in. flowers are creamy white, and the stems are tinged purple. Tall meadow rue (*T. pubescens*; 3-7 ft. × 2-3 ft.), sometimes called "king of the meadow," displays plumes of starry, 1/3-in. white flowers in midsummer, and makes an excellent addition to rain gardens. Rue-anemone (*T. thalictroides*, formerly classified as *Anemonella thalictroides*; 6-9 in. × 6-9 in.) has foliage resembling that of the above species, but is monoecious, having both male and female parts within the same flower. It blooms in white

Thalictrum dioicum adds effervescence to the early spring garden.

(sometimes pink to deep pink) with flowers that lack petals and are composed of five to ten showy, petal-like sepals surrounding a central boss of stamens.

Rue-anemone lacks nectar, but attracts pollinating insects, and although summer dormant, it is a charming spring woodland wildflower. Neither rabbits nor deer feed on any of these species. With the exception of the last, meadow rues are fine middle- to back-of-the-border plants, and make quite a statement, especially in partly shaded woodland, native plant, pollinator, and wildlife gardens.

CULTURE AND TIPS

Early meadow rue thrives in shaded or partly shaded places where soil remains moist. It will adapt to sunnier positions as long as the soil does not dry out in summer. Divide established plants in spring, or start seed outdoors in fall and overwinter. Powdery mildew and rust sometimes become problems, especially in drier soils. This plant can be successfully refreshed during the growing season by cutting it back entirely to the ground in summer, prompting it to send up new growth within two weeks.

Thalictrum thalictroides is another gardenworthy, deer-resistant perennial for early spring.

COMPANION PLANTS

In woodlands, partner early meadow rue with spring wildflowers such as its cousin, rue-anemone (*Thalictrum thalictroides*); wild bleeding heart (*Dicentra eximia*); green-and-gold (*Chrysogonum virginianum*); red columbine (*Aquilegia canadensis*); and annuals purple phacelia (*Phacelia bipinnatifida*) and blue-eyed Mary (*Collinsia verna*). All bloom roughly over the same period. For foliar complement, try ostrich fern (*Matteuccia struthiopteris*).

DID YOU KNOW?

The leaves of early meadow rue appear silver when placed in water, hence the common name quicksilver weed. Meadow rue is wind-pollinated, therefore the species of bees that visit seek the pollen available only from the male flowers, since there is no nectar to be found. It is a larval host food for borer and Canadian owlet moths, among others, which lay their eggs on the leaves. The Skagit tribe of the Northwest are said to have used boiled leaves of rue anemone to make a hair wash.

Vernonia noveboracensis DAISY FAMILY (ASTERACEAE)
New York ironweed

DEER RESISTANCE	HARDINESS ZONES	NORTHEAST NATIVE STATES	HEIGHT/SPREAD
9–10	5–9	CT, DC, DE, MA, MD, NH, NJ, NY, PA, RI, VA, WV	4–5 FT. × 3–4 FT.

Vernonia noveboracensis blooms in brilliant magenta purple.

Large and vigorous, New York ironweed makes a colorful statement for gardeners and pollinators in late summer. Its tall, strong stems branch toward the top and support loose, flat-topped clusters of brilliant purple, fluffy flower heads—a delight for all. These are composed of clusters of individual, tubular disk flowers that lack ray petals. Slender, dark green, lance-shaped leaves are arranged alternately on the stiff, purplish green stems. Perhaps due to its size, this excellent perennial is underused in residential gardens, but should be featured more often.

The cultivar 'White Lightning' (5–6 ft. × 2½–3 ft.) has pure white, almost feathery-looking flowers. Thread-leaf ironweed (*V. lettermannii*)

(2½–3 ft. × 2-2½ ft.) is another excellent species, and its cultivar 'Iron Butterfly' (2-3 ft. × 2-3 ft.) is outstanding in the garden. The latter has become very popular for its long bloom time, fine narrow foliage, and the familiar butterfly-attracting purple flowers. 'Summer's Swan Song' (2½–3½ ft. × 3-3½ ft.) is another great garden cultivar, the result of a cross between *V. lettermannii* and *V. angustifolia* 'Plum Peachy'. Yet another selection of merit is 'Summer's Surrender' (*V. lettermannii* × *V. arkansana*; 3-4 ft. × 5-6 ft.), which features linear, dark green, mildew-resistant leaves and late summer blooms of dark purple. All are appropriate for naturalizing in butterfly and pollinator gardens, as well as rain gardens. When massed, ironweed's vast roots can be useful in holding soil to control erosion. The smaller selections are perfect for residential beds and borders, and all species tolerate the negative effects of black walnut trees.

CULTURE AND TIPS

New York ironweed thrives in full sun, and grows best in medium to wet soils of average fertility. However, it does well in a wide range of soils, preferably those on the acidic side. In the wild, it is often found streamside, and in moist meadows and sunny swales where soil remains wet in summer. If ironweed gets too tall for its neighbors, cut to half height in late spring—it will still bloom well, and at a more modest height. Staking can be beneficial, especially in a more structured garden setting. Sometimes powdery mildew and rust become

aesthetic issues for foliage, but do not affect the plant's overall performance. When placed in the garden, ironweed benefits from free air circulation, as it reduces the chance of mildew. Cut back as necessary after bloom to reduce self-seeding, but leave some stems for birds to enjoy the seed, for overwintering nests for beneficial insects, and as perches for migratory birds in early spring. Direct sow seeds in fall, or stratify for spring sowing indoors. Ironweed may be divided in early spring, and divisions must be kept watered until they are well established.

COMPANION PLANTS

Although late in the season to bloom, this imposing giant earns its keep among others that enjoy damp conditions. Spotted Joe-Pye weed (*Eutrochium maculatum*), great blue lobelia (*Lobelia siphilitica*), Cardinal flower (*Lobelia cardinalis*), and cutleaf coneflower (*Rudbeckia laciniata*) are excellent companions in the garden, just as they grow in the wild. Try blue mistflower (*Conoclinium coelestinum*) and swamp milkweed (*Asclepias incarnata*) to start the bloom season earlier.

DID YOU KNOW?

At one time, the long, fibrous stems of ironweed were used as packing to transport whiskey bottles safely. Many butterflies, including skippers, are attracted to its flowers, and it is the host plant for American painted lady caterpillars. Many species of native bees and non-native honeybees flock to this plant for nectar in late summer.

Vernonia lettermannii has fuzzy flowers and foliage. Shown here is the popular cultivar 'Iron Butterfly'.

Ferns

Ferns are a group of ancient plants that are unique in that they don't produce flowers, but reproduce by spores, vegetative means, or both. They're well known for their leaves, called fronds, which come in various sizes, shapes, and arrangements, depending upon the type of fern. These varying shapes add interest to the landscape, and contrast well with flowering annuals, biennials, perennials, and shrubs. Ferns are the stalwarts of the shade garden, and besides their reliability, their most enviable trait for our purposes is the fact that deer rarely, if ever, feed upon them. Fawns may occasionally sample tender new growth, but deer generally do not care for the taste of ferns, and otherwise leave them alone.

We have selected five ferns that, in our experience, provide excellent additions to shade or part-sun gardens.

Adiantum pedatum BRAKE FERN FAMILY (PTERIDACEAE)

Northern maidenhair fern

DEER RESISTANCE	HARDINESS ZONES	NORTHEAST NATIVE STATES	HEIGHT/SPREAD
9-10	3-8	CT, DC, DE, MA, MD, ME, NH, NJ, NY, PA, RI, VA, VT, WV	18-24 IN. × 18-24 IN.

Of the many native ferns available in the marketplace, northern maidenhair is one of the most distinctive in shape and appearance. Supported by black stems (correctly called stipes), its fronds are held parallel to the ground,

Maidenhair fern's fronds make an alluring addition to the summer shade garden.

rather than vertically. In spring, when fronds first emerge, they transition in shape and color, changing each day until mature. Each individual frond features a group of many smaller leaflets that have a delicate appearance, and flutter in the breeze. Plants develop into tight clumps. This species is an excellent, unique choice for shade gardens, especially when planted near the bases of larger shrubs.

CULTURE AND TIPS

Like many other ferns, maidenhair thrives in part to full shade and moist, well-drained soil, high in organic matter. Surprisingly, once established, this fern tolerates some drought too. Some fronds may deteriorate as the growing season progresses, depending upon conditions. These, however, can be cut to ground level, and new fronds will appear within a short time.

Adiantum pedatum has a unique look among ferns.

COMPANION PLANTS

Other ferns, particularly common lady fern (*Athyrium filix-femina*), provide differently textured foliage from maidenhair ferns, as does silver sedge (*Carex platyphylla*). The bright flowers of annual blue-eyed Mary (*Collinsia verna*) and green-and-gold (*Chrysogonum virginianum*), along with white-flowered rue-anemone (*Thalictrum thalictroides*) and tall early meadow rue (*Thalictrum dioicum*), make good companions for color in wood-lands, as well as shaded beds and borders. Long-blooming wild bleeding heart (*Dicentra eximia*) provides foliar color contrast with its grayish green leaves, and thrives under similar cultural conditions.

DID YOU KNOW?

The tiny pinnae (leaflets) on this fern's fronds are shaped like a hand fan, much like those of the Asian maidenhair tree (*Gingko biloba*), from which the plant's common name is derived.

133

Athyrium filix-femina WOOD FERN FAMILY (DRYOPTERIDACEAE)

Northern lady fern

DEER RESISTANCE	HARDINESS ZONES	NORTHEAST NATIVE STATES	HEIGHT/SPREAD
9-10	4-8	CT, DC, DE, MA, MD, ME, NH, NJ, NY, PA, RI, VA, VT, WV	12-18 IN. × 18-24 IN.

Attractive northern lady fern is one of the easiest ferns to grow. It forms dense clumps of upright, lacey foliage that dies down in winter. Its stipes (stems) are typically green, however there is a naturally occurring form that features red stipes, unique within the fern world. 'Lady in Red' is a cultivar of this form. The fine-textured foliage is refreshing in shade gardens in summer, adding interest at a time of year when it is most needed. Lady fern widens its clumps gently over time, but never gets too large for its space. The delicate foliage contrasts well with other plants with bolder leaves. This fern is an excellent choice for shade in-ground or in containers.

CULTURE AND TIPS

Low-maintenance northern lady fern prefers part to full shade and moist, well-drained soil high in organic matter, preferably on the acidic side. That said, once it's established, this fern is fairly drought tolerant, although it performs best with additional watering during hot, dry periods. It refreshes well in summer—that is, if some fronds start to fade, prune them to near ground level, and new fronds will replace them in a few weeks. To increase stock, divided older clumps in early spring, and water well until established.

Athyrium filix-femina is easy to grow and adaptable.

COMPANION PLANTS

Mix northern lady fern with spring-blooming woodland plants such as green-and-gold (*Chrysogonum virginianum*), Canada anemone (*Anemone canadensis*), and biennial purple phacelia (*Phacelia bipinnatafida*). Marginal wood fern (*Dryopteris marginalis*) and maidenhair fern (*Adiantum pedatum*) are excellent companions as well.

DID YOU KNOW?

Lady fern's common name comes from the fact that the structures that produce and contain the fern's spores, called sori, are crescent-shaped, and thought to resemble a woman's eyebrows.

Dryopteris marginalis WOOD FERN FAMILY (DRYOPTERIDACEAE)

Marginal wood fern, leatherwood fern

DEER RESISTANCE	HARDINESS ZONES	NORTHEAST NATIVE STATES	HEIGHT/SPREAD
9-10	2-8	CT, DC, DE, MA, MD, ME, NH, NJ, NY, PA, RI, VA, VT, WV	24-36 IN. × 24-36 IN.

Wood ferns are some of the best and most reliable ferns for shade gardens as they are adaptable and long-lived. Marginal wood fern is a prime choice for deer resistance and general reliability. Medium-green, upright fronds form a cylindrical whorl, and create the familiar vase shape. This fern's best attributes include extreme cold hardiness and the ability to tolerate drought, especially in woodlands during dry summers.

Three other wood ferns well worth considering are deciduous Goldie's wood fern (*Dryopteris goldiana*; 3-4 ft. × 3-4 ft.), semi-evergreen dixie wood fern (*D. ×australis*; 4-5 ft. × 2-3 ft.), and evergreen intermediate wood fern (*D. intermedia*; 1-3 ft. × 1-3 ft.). Goldie's wood fern, with its shiny, dark green, 3- to 4-ft. high fronds, is one of the largest of the group. It makes sizable clumps, and is ideal as a backdrop for other, smaller plants. Similarly-sized dixie wood fern has erect, paler green fronds. Its vigorous clumps also increase in size to make a showy statement. Intermediate wood fern has medium-green fronds that are more delicate in appearance.

CULTURE AND TIPS

Wood fern requires well-drained soils, but adapts to a wide range of soil types, including acidic, neutral, and slightly alkaline. It prefers moist soils high in organic matter. Once established, marginal and intermediate wood ferns tolerate short periods of drought well. All benefit from a natural mulch of leaf debris to help

Dryopteris marginalis is one of the most drought-tolerant ferns.

conserve soil moisture, add organic matter, and support healthy soil microbes that contribute to the ferns' success.

COMPANION PLANTS

Both green-and-gold (*Chrysogonum virginianum*) and rue anemone (*Thalictrum thalictroides*) serve well as underplantings for marginal wood fern. It works well with tall meadow-rue (*Thalictrum pubescens*), spreading sedge (*Carex laxiculmis*), and wild bleeding heart (*Dicentra eximia*). Northern lady fern (*Athyrium filix-femina*) is also a fine companion.

DID YOU KNOW?

A combination of different species of wood ferns creates an attractive feature in summer shade gardens, especially during the period when many flowering plants lack color. They bring a sense of lushness so many gardeners love in a woodland setting.

Matteuccia struthiopteris   SENSITIVE FERN FAMILY (ONOCLEACEAE)

Ostrich fern

DEER RESISTANCE	HARDINESS ZONES	NORTHEAST NATIVE STATES	HEIGHT/SPREAD
8-10	3-8	CT, DC, MA, MD, ME, NH, NJ, NY, PA, RI, VA, VT, WV	24-48 IN. × 24-36 IN.

Ostrich fern has both sterile and fertile fronds.

Ostrich fern is one of the best choices for moist to wet, shady spots in woodland gardens, and its emerging fronds in spring are a sight to behold. This fern has two types of fronds: one sterile, the other fertile. Its sterile fronds produce whorls of vase-shaped crowns, and these are the fronds we admire most. Their role is to photosynthesize and produce food for the plant. Fertile fronds' sole purpose is to produce spores, which is how ferns reproduce sexually. The fertile fronds' structures persist well into winter, turning a deep brown color, and provide interest long after sterile fronds have faded.

Under favorable conditions, this fern can be somewhat aggressive, however it's an excellent choice for large areas, especially low, wet spots. It spreads by underground runners called stolons,

Matteuccia struthiopteris is easy and quick to establish, especially in moist, woodland conditions.

which create extensive, fibrous root systems, and aid in soil stabilization. That makes this fern a valuable asset in controlling erosion along streambanks, and effective in rain gardens. Its ease of culture is one of its best attributes.

CULTURE AND TIPS

Ostrich fern thrives in moist, rich soil, and excels in areas near streams in high shade, and even in full sun with moist conditions. Late in summer, its fronds start to yellow and fade, but they can be cut back to the ground for tidiness with no adverse effect on the next season's growth.

COMPANION PLANTS

In spring, wild bleeding heart (*Dicentra eximia*) brightens up shade gardens at the feet of developing ostrich fern. For interest a little later, combine ostrich fern with other tall, shade-loving perennials, including red columbine (*Aquilegia canadensis*), Canada anemone (*Anemone canadensis*), and early meadow rue (*Thalictrum dioicum*). In sunnier situations, a stand of summer-blooming species such as blue mistflower (*Conoclinum coelestinum*), cardinal flower (*Lobelia cardinalis*), and great blue lobelia (*L. siphilitica*) gains another dimension when combined with bold ostrich fern fronds.

DID YOU KNOW?

In spring, ostrich fern produces edible fiddle-heads that, when cooked, are a delicacy used in a variety of savory dishes like soups, quiches, and omelets. A fern we can eat, but deer will not!

Polystichum acrostichoides WOOD FERN FAMILY (DRYOPTERIDACEAE)
Christmas fern

DEER RESISTANCE	HARDINESS ZONES	NORTHEAST NATIVE STATES	HEIGHT/SPREAD
8-10	3-9	CT, DC, DE, MA, MD, ME, NH, NJ, NY, PA, RI, VA, VT, WV	12-24 IN. × 12-24 IN.

Christmas fern is appealing and distinctive as well as long-lived, and it deserves a place in every shade garden. It has year-round appeal with its furry stipes (stems) and evergreen fronds that make it a perfect companion for many of our woodland plants. In the wild, individual clumps may occur by the hundreds on north-facing hillsides. Christmas fern is most content on shady, wooded slopes and at the base of trees, where it is a welcome sight, especially in winter. Its evergreen fronds add a dimension of seasonal interest in addition to helping hold leaf debris in place that acts as mulch. Its fine root system helps stabilize soil.

CULTURE AND TIPS

Christmas fern prefers a moist, acid, well-drained soil high in organic matter, and part to full shade. Once established, this fern tolerates drought well. Offsets arise from its rhizomes, and these can be dug, divided, and replanted successfully in mid- to late spring. Make sure to provide sufficient moisture for several months until plants are well established. Though some gardeners like to trim the previous season's growth off in early spring for neatness, this really isn't necessary, as newly emerging growth quickly hides the old.

Polystichum acrostichoides is an evergreen fern perfectly sited in shade.

COMPANION PLANTS

Dress up Christmas fern with low-growing, early-blooming species. Try biennial purple phacelia (*Phacelia bipinnatifida*) for a splash of color. Rue anemone (*Thalictrum thalictroides*) and red columbine (*Aquilegia canadesis*) work well, as does the matte green foliage of wild ginger (*Asarum canadensis*), which also emerges early. The foliage of marginal wood fern (*Dryopteris marginalis*) also contrasts well with that of Christmas fern.

DID YOU KNOW?

Evergreen Christmas fern earned its common name as it was traditionally used for holiday greens for decoration. Additionally, the individual L-shaped pinnae (leaflets) are thought to resemble Christmas stockings.

Grasses

Typically, grasses are known as leafy plants for foliar interest. Their flowers, however, are an important component to their appearance in the landscape. Called inflorescences, these flowering structures shine especially late summer into winter. A good example of this is muhly grass (*Muhlenbergia capillaris*), whose early fall display of pink inflorescences absolutely steals the show in the fall garden.

Our native grasses have many redeeming features, including hardiness and tolerance of heat, drought, and poor soil, as well as ease of care and maintenance. Their most redeeming feature may be that deer rarely, if ever, feed on them. When used effectively in the garden, grasses provide a unique appearance that contrasts well with annuals, perennials, and shrubs. They also provide multi-season interest from late spring all the way through winter, a season when most other plants in the landscape are dormant. We have chosen five native grasses to recommend based upon our experience with them in the garden.

Deschampsia cespitosa GRASS FAMILY (POACEAE)

Tufted hair grass

DEER RESISTANCE	HARDINESS ZONES	NORTHEAST NATIVE STATES	HEIGHT/SPREAD
9-10	4-9	CT, MA, MD, ME, NH, NJ, NY, PA, VA, VT, WV	10-16 IN. × 12-24 IN.

Tufted hair grass features hundreds of 2-ft. long, narrow, semi-evergreen leaves that are upright to arching, and arranged in dense clumps. In midsummer, numerous flower stems emerge, rising above the foliage and to a height of roughly 3 ft. The stems feature wide, billowy panicles of miniature, multicolored flowers in varying shades of gold, green, and purple. These flower stems persist for months, bringing movement to the garden when the most gentle breeze blows. After the flowers fade and set seed, they provide structural interest lasting well into winter.

CULTURE AND TIPS

This cool-season grass thrives in full sun, where it flowers best, but also adapts well to part shade, and is one of the best cool-season grasses for lower light conditions. Tufted hair grass performs well farther north and is hardy to zone 4, though it also persists through the hot, humid conditions of the mid-Atlantic region. Well-drained, moisture-retentive soils are best, but it also tolerates some drought once it's established. This grass is an excellent addition to any meadow edge, or massed in beds and borders. When used only a few at a time in a group, repeat these groups throughout the border to carry the characteristic effect of its airy inflorescences throughout the design.

COMPANION PLANTS

Tufted hair grass is a nice addition with other hardy grasses, and its unique look complements herbaceous flowering plants such as star tickseed (*Coreopsis pubescens*), purple coneflower (*Echinacea purpurea*), and wild bergamot (*Monarda fistulosa*). In sunnier gardens, tufted hair grass can be interplanted with Virginia sweetspire (*Itea virginica*), red chokeberry (*Aronia arbutifolia*), and American beautyberry (*Callicarpa americana*).

DID YOU KNOW?

The common name tufted hair grass refers to this plant's many fine, hair-like leaves arranged in a mounding tuft.

Deschampsia cespitosa tolerates partial shade, and does well in among garden perennials.

Muhlenbergia capillaris GRASS FAMILY (POACEAE)

Muhly grass, pink muhly grass

DEER RESISTANCE	HARDINESS ZONES	NORTHEAST NATIVE STATES	HEIGHT/SPREAD
9-10	5-9	CT, DC, DE, MA, MD, NJ, NY, PA, VA, WV	2-3 FT. × 2-3 FT.

In bloom, muhly grass is by far one of the most attractive and memorable of our native grasses. This warm-season grass features hundreds of narrow, almost thread-like leaves in dark green, which form dense clumps and provide a soft— dare we say fluffy—texture in the garden. Muhly grass is unique among grasses in that it blooms in mid-fall, with billowy, brilliantly striking inflorescences of bright rosy pink. Garden visitors frequently exclaim "What is that?!" with surprise and delight. The blooms effervesce above the dark foliage much like a pink cloud for several weeks. Once flowering ceases, the stems and beige seed plumes persist for months, into late fall and winter, adding movement to the garden at every breeze.

White-flowered cultivar 'White Cloud' (3-4 ft. × 3-4 ft.) is somewhat larger, with breathtaking flower heads that appear like pools of moonlight in the landscape, a surreal effect, especially at dusk. Muhly grass is valuable for adding seasonal interest in summer, fall, and winter.

Indispensable in any meadow garden, muhly grass works equally en masse as in smaller numbers in beds and borders. Its airy pink inflorescences are unforgettable, and seem to be nature's way of making a grand final statement as the growing season draws to a close.

CULTURE AND TIPS

This warm-season grass thrives in full sun in a wide range of soils, including sandy and gravelly ones, as long as they drain well. Keep it watered when young—once established, muhly grass is very drought tolerant. Rich soils that are overly moist yield larger plants, yet these are seldom as sturdy as those grown in leaner soils. After winter, cut down clumps before new

Muhly grass is exceptionally beautiful in fall when it comes into bloom, and makes quite a statement en masse.

growth emerges. Increase by division of mature plants. Muhly grass performs flawlessly in areas with hot, humid summers.

COMPANION PLANTS

Muhly grass combines well with other hardy grasses such as prairie dropseed (*Sporobolus heterolepis*) and switchgrass (*Panicum virgatum*), and can be utilized in endless combinations. Flowering perennials like diminutive smallhead blazing star (*Liatris microcephala*), shrub-like azure blue sage (*Salvia azurea* var. *grandiflora*), and imposing prairie rosinweed (*Silphium terebinthinaceum*) add interest and contrast in size, texture, and form. Two compatible shrubs include red chokeberry (*Aronia arbutifolia*) and American beautyberry (*Callicarpa americana*), whose berries also add late season interest.

DID YOU KNOW?

The genus name of *Muhlenbergia* celebrates Lutheran pastor and amateur botanist Gottlief Henry Ernest Muhlenberg (1753–1815).

147

Panicum virgatum GRASS FAMILY (POACEAE)

Switchgrass

DEER RESISTANCE	HARDINESS ZONES	NORTHEAST NATIVE STATES	HEIGHT/SPREAD
9-10	5-9	CT, DC, DE, MA, MD, ME, NH, NJ, NY, PA, RI, VA, VT, WV	3-6 FT. × 2-3 FT.

Switchgrass is a dependable and highly adaptable plant with many cultivars, including 'Cloud Nine', shown here.

Switchgrass is very dependable, easily grown, and site-adaptable, making it a must-have in almost any garden type and situation. This warm-season ornamental grass features hundreds of narrow, ½-in. wide, medium green leaves that form sizable upright clumps. Delicate, plumy panicles of bloom rise above arching foliage in midsummer. Once flowering ceases, these are loaded with tannish beige seedheads that persist for months into late fall and winter. Leaves also turn yellow in fall, often with reddish tips, and slowly transition to tan over winter. The persistent seedheads are an important winter food source for wild birds.

Some excellent cultivars of switchgrass include the strong, upright 'Northwind' (4-5 ft. × 2-3 ft.) from Roy Diblik's Northwind Perennial

Panicum virgatum features upright foliage and airy flowers.

Farm; compact and vase-shaped 'Shenandoah' (3-4 ft. × 3-4 ft.), with reddish tinged leaves and rosy pink inflorescences; and upright but more compact 'Cape Breeze' (2-2½ ft. × 1½-2 ft.). Switchgrass's adaptability to adverse conditions is among its best attributes, making it highly desirable in almost any garden situation. Consider planting it at the back of perennial borders, as a seasonal foundation plant in home landscapes, as a specimen in mixed beds, even in parking lot areas where salt is used to mitigate ice in winter.

CULTURE AND TIPS

This warm-season grass thrives in full sun to part shade in an incredibly wide range of soils, from acidic and wet to lean, dry, upland soils. It tolerates salty conditions well, making it especially useful in areas from coastal gardens to median strips treated with salt in winter. Very little maintenance is necessary except to trim its old leaves to the ground between late winter and early spring. Although switchgrass will grow in part shade, it tends to flop, with less vigorous and structured growth.

COMPANION PLANTS

Switchgrass combines well with so many plants offering contrasting texture, shape, and size. Try prairie dropseed (*Sporobolus heterolepis*) and muhly grass (*Muhlenbergia capillaris*) for additional grass combinations. Perennial companions include mountain mint (*Pycnanthemum muticum*), azure blue sage (*Salvia azurea* var. *grandiflora*), wild bergamot (*Monarda fistulosa*) and Maryland senna (*Senna marilandica*) for added interest and contrast. Recommended shrubs to combine with switchgrass include northern bayberry (*Morella pensylvanica*), American beautyberry (*Callicarpa americana*), and arrowwood viburnum (*Viburnum dentatum*).

DID YOU KNOW?

Switchgrass not only provides seed for winter-foraging birds, but also protective cover and nesting material in spring. The cultivar 'Northwind' was named the 2014 perennial plant of the year by the Perennial Plant Association.

Schizachyrium scoparium GRASS FAMILY (POACEAE)
Little bluestem

DEER RESISTANCE	HARDINESS ZONES	NORTHEAST NATIVE STATES	HEIGHT/SPREAD
9-10	3-9	CT, DC, DE, MA, MD, ME, NH, NJ, NY, PA, RI, VA, VT, WV	2-4 FT. × 1½-2 FT.

Seedheads of little bluestem are attractive all winter.

Little bluestem is truly one of the most durable and long-lived choices of the many native grasses, as well as one of the most widespread—it can be found in 48 states. This warm-season, clump-forming grass features narrow, ¼-in. wide basal leaves of medium green, often tinged with blue, and in some forms, pigmented with red and purple. It is well known for its fall color. In midsummer, its habit becomes more upright as its bloom-stalks form, growing to 3 to 4 ft. The plumy blooms show off silvery white seedheads that persist into winter, and early into the following spring, delivering a long season of interest, and providing an important source of food for birds.

There are many outstanding and colorful cultivars of little bluestem, including the strong, upright 'Standing Ovation' (2-4 ft. × 1-2 ft.), with its unmistakable, purplish bronze coloring and superlatively vertical growth; decidedly blue-tinted 'The Blues' (2-4 ft. × 1½-2 ft.); and 'Blaze' (2-3 ft. × 1½-2 ft.), with blue-green summer foliage and outstanding fall color in a mix of reds, purples, oranges, and pinks. Little bluestem seems indifferent to drought, heat, humidity, and poor soils, which makes it successful in almost any garden or site.

CULTURE AND TIPS

This warm-season grass thrives in full sun in a wide range of soils, from acidic to alkaline, lean, and dry. It performs best in low-nutrient soils, as richer soils result in luxuriant growth that tends to tip and flop. Very little maintenance is necessary except to trim its old leaves and stems to the ground between late winter and early spring. It can spread rather vigorously by seeding about, so regular weeding to keep it in check is advisable.

COMPANION PLANTS

Little bluestem combines well with many other sun-loving grasses, such as prairie dropseed (*Sporobolus heterolepis*) and pink muhly grass (*Muhlenbergia capillaris*), as well as perennials including azure blue sage (*Salvia azurea* var. *grandiflora*), and Maryland senna (*Senna marilandica*). There are many shrubs recommended to combine with little bluestem. Excellent choices being northern bayberry (*Morella pensylvanica*) and American beautyberry (*Callicarpa americana*).

DID YOU KNOW?

Little bluestem is one of the very first native grasses to establish itself in open areas of disturbance, as well as the first to appear after wildfires. It is a first succession plant in the evolution of a site, from bare earth to meadow and then woodland.

Schizachyrium scoparium is as effective on its own in a perennial border as en masse in a meadow.

Sporobolus heterolepis GRASS FAMILY (POACEAE)

Prairie dropseed

DEER RESISTANCE	HARDINESS ZONES	NORTHEAST NATIVE STATES	HEIGHT/SPREAD
9–10	3–9	CT, MA, MD, NY, PA, VA	2–3 FT. × 2–3 FT.

Prairie dropseed offers another easy-to-grow, undemanding, and attractive option among native grasses for use in the garden. This warm-season, clumping grass features

Inflorescences of prairie dropseed are as ethereal as its soft foliage, and smell very much like popcorn.

hundreds of fine-textured, almost thread-like, medium green leaves that form dense masses with a soft, billowy texture. Open and arching panicles of pale brown and pink appear in late summer, 30 to 36 in. above the mass of leaves. These inflorescences are best known for their unique fragrance, which many consider reminiscent of popcorn or perhaps coriander. In fall, the foliage transitions in color to orange-gold and then pale bronze. In winter, the remaining flower stalks turn golden brown and persist well into the colder months.

CULTURE AND TIPS

Prairie dropseed thrives in full sun in a wide range of soils, including those of very hot and dry areas, which make this grass indispensable for use in meadows, restored prairies, and dry slopes. Keep it watered when first planted, but once established, it is very drought tolerant, and does not require additional watering even in extended dry periods. Rich soils should be

Sporobolus heterolepis adds an incredible dimension of softness and lushness to any garden setting.

avoided. Used en masse, this grass can be stunning, and is the perfect filler for hot, sunny areas such as medians, and areas near pavement or roadways. After winter, some choose to cut down the golden leaves, but many find it unnecessary, as this grass thrives regardless. Prairie dropseed can be started successfully from seed, but it grows slowly, requiring several years to reach maturity. Patience is a virtue with this grass as it matures and settles in, but once it does, it's very long-lived.

COMPANION PLANTS

Prairie dropseed makes an excellent companion for other native grasses such as pink muhly grass (*Muhlenbergia capillaris*) and switchgrass (*Panicum virgatum*), and there is no limit to the possible combinations. Flowering perennial companions include smallhead blazing star (*Liatris microcephala*), drought-tolerant azure blue sage (*Salvia azurea* var. *grandiflora*), and attractive Simpson's rosinweed (*Silphium simpsonii*), which add interest and contrast in size, texture, and form. Two shrubs that are recommended are red chokeberry (*Aronia arbutifolia*) and American beautyberry (*Callicarpa americana*), whose berries peak simultaneously with prairie dropseed's foliage color transition.

DID YOU KNOW?

The common name of this grass is derived from the fact that the small, rounded seeds drop from their hulls in fall.

Sedges

Sedges are grass-like plants with triangular stems in the plant family Cyperaceae, and they are widely distributed throughout most of the world. Many members of this family have "sedge" as part of their common names, but we are specifically focusing on the genus *Carex*. Its species are the physical archetype for sedges, and are thus known as "true sedges."

There are over 2,000 species of *Carex* adapted to grow in many different situations, from dry and shady, wet and sunny, and everything else in between. These plants are best known for their foliage, while their flowers (called inflorescences) are typically inconspicuous. Many shade-loving sedges are valuable woodland plants. Along with ferns, they bring interest and contrast to gardens with lower light, especially in summer and fall, when other flowering plants have finished their floral display or gone dormant altogether. Like ferns, sedges are rarely, if ever, bothered by deer, making them yet more valuable for use in the garden. We have selected five sedges we recommend based upon our gardening experience with them.

Carex appalachica SEDGE FAMILY (CYPERACEAE)

Appalachian sedge

DEER RESISTANCE	HARDINESS ZONES	NORTHEAST NATIVE STATES	HEIGHT/SPREAD
9-10	3-8	CT, MA, MD, ME, NH, NJ, NY, PA, VA, VT, WV	10-12 IN. × 10-12 IN.

Appalachian sedge forms small, dense clumps of hundreds of 12-in. long, bright green leaves, arching and very fine, almost wiry. These clumps are highly valued for adding a grass-like effect in shady, woodland gardens. In spring, they produce small stems holding minute inflorescences, which may be singly insignificant, but add a dimension of airiness in large numbers not often found in any other plants.

The foliage brings softness to naturalistic gardens, a delicate effect wherever it is planted, especially at the bases of larger plants or shrubs. Because of its diminutive size, this plant is also prized for use in container plantings and small troughs. Nothing is more effective to contrast the bold leaves of other plants than Appalachian sedge.

CULTURE AND TIPS

Appalachian sedge thrives in light to medium shade, in dry to moist, well-drained soil high in organic matter. It is the type of sedge that forms clumps, so its crown is composed of many single plants and can easily be separated and divided. These small clumps can be replanted successfully, and will enlarge over a few seasons—an effective means to increase this worthwhile sedge in your garden. Planted in its ideal habitat, Appalachian sedge will also reseed and spread. As with all sedges, keep divisions or seedlings well-watered until they are established. At planting time, the addition of finely shredded leaf mulch is beneficial to add organic matter to the soil, aid in conserving water, and reduce variations in soil temperature across the four seasons.

CAREX APPALACHICA

Carex appalachica softens almost any shady spot with its narrow, grass-like foliage.

COMPANION PLANTS

Appalachian sedge is nicely complemented by green-and-gold (*Chrysogonum virginianum*), Indian pink (*Spigelia marilandica*), and purple phacelia (*Phacelia bipinnatifida*). This sedge contrasts well with the bold, dark green foliage of wild ginger (*Asarum canadense*) and Christmas fern (*Polystichum acrostichoides*). Use it as an understory planting with New Jersey tea (*Ceanothus americanus*), American beautyberry (*Callicarpa americana*), and inkberry (*Ilex glabra*).

DID YOU KNOW?

Appalachian sedge is considered an effective lawn alternative for areas where it can be planted en masse and undisturbed by foot traffic, mowing, and fertilizing.

Carex laxiculmis SEDGE FAMILY (CYPERACEAE)
Spreading sedge, creeping sedge

DEER RESISTANCE	HARDINESS ZONES	NORTHEAST NATIVE STATES	HEIGHT/SPREAD
9-10	5-9	CT, MA, MD, ME, NH, NJ, NY, PA, VA, VT, WV	6-12 IN. × 6-10 IN.

Spreading sedge displays narrow, ½-in. wide, ridged leaves, each with a furrowed midrib, arranged in wide rosettes. These rosettes form whorls of bluish green foliage with a silvery cast.

This sedge thrives in light to medium shade, and is a welcome addition for spots of cool color in naturalistic gardens, near walkways, at the bases of larger plants and shrubs, and nearly any other spot where its leaf clusters can add contrast to bolder colors and textures. A very popular cultivar is 'Hobb' (also called 'Bunny Blue'). It is known for its pronounced, bright blue foliage color, supposedly more so than that of the typical species.

CULTURE AND TIPS

Spreading sedge thrives in partly shaded locations, in rich, consistently moist soil high in organic matter. As with many clumping sedges, it grows as a tight crown composed of many single plants, and large clumps can easily be separated and divided into smaller ones. The small clumps can be replanted successfully, and will enlarge over a few seasons. Spreading sedge is also known to reseed readily, and relocating young plants is a quick method to increasing this excellent plant. Make sure to water newly transplanted divisions and seedlings well until they are established. An application of finely shredded leaf mulch is beneficial, not only for adding organic matter to the soil, but also for conserving water and keeping soil temperatures cooler in summer.

COMPANION PLANTS

Spreading sedge is nicely complemented by wild bleeding heart (*Dicentra eximia*), green-and-gold (*Chrysogonum virginianum*), and Indian pink (*Spigelia marilandica*). This sedge makes

Carex laxiculmis features whorls of bluish green foliage, especially cultivar 'Hobb' or Bunny Blue, shown here.

an excellent understory planting for various shrubs such as mapleleaf viburnum (*Viburnum acerifolium*), devilwood (*Osmanthus americanus*), and New Jersey tea (*Ceanothus americanus*), and complements the stunning magenta fruit of American beautyberry (*Callicarpa americana*) especially well.

DID YOU KNOW?

Though found in shade in nature, spreading sedge will perform well in full sun as long as soil is not allowed to dry out.

Carex pensylvanica SEDGE FAMILY (CYPERACEAE)
Pennsylvania sedge, oak sedge

DEER RESISTANCE	HARDINESS ZONES	NORTHEAST NATIVE STATES	HEIGHT/SPREAD
9-10	3-8	CT, MA, MD, ME, NH, NJ, NY, PA, VA, VT, WV	6-12 IN. × 10-15 IN.

Pennsylvania sedge features narrow, ⅛-in. wide, semi-evergreen leaves of medium green, which arise from multiple spreading rhizomes. These form large masses, making the plant an effective groundcover. Pennsylvania sedge thrives in light to medium shade, and its ability to spread and create sizable masses has made it a welcome species in the dry shade of deciduous trees, especially in areas where many other plants struggle. The soft appearance of its fine, grassy foliage adds a unique aesthetic to naturalistic gardens, softening areas along paths, or massed in open woodland situations, whether under one tree or many.

CULTURE AND TIPS

This sedge is easy to grow in moist to dry, well-drained, organic soils in part to full shade, though more light produces quicker growth overall. It also grows well in clay loams. Due to Pennsylvania sedge's ability to spread well in shade, it has been effectively utilized as a replacement for non-native lawn grasses where foot traffic is infrequent. It can be allowed to grow to its ultimate height of 6 to 12 in., or trimmed to roughly 2 in. high once or twice during the growing season. Because it's difficult from seed, the best way to increase this plant is by division. Though drought tolerant once established, newly transplanted divisions should be kept well-watered for the remainder of that growing season. Though other sedges benefit from a light mulch of finely shredded leaves in fall, Pennsylvania sedge tolerates open, sun-dappled ground with little or no leaf litter. It is often sited on hilltops or slopes where leaves tend not to collect. It has also been used effectively in containers as a fine-foliage accent to larger plants with bolder leaves.

COMPANION PLANTS

Pennsylvania sedge makes an excellent base layer next to or under other plants. Combine it with lady fern (*Athyrium filix-femina*), or try marginal wood fern (*Dryopteris marginalis*) in drier upland situations under trees. For additional flowering companions, the fine leaf texture of this sedge is stunning with wild bleeding heart

Carex pensylvanica makes an excellent foliage plant, especially to soften edges of paths.

(*Dicentra eximia*), rue-anemone (*Thalictrum thalictroides*), and red columbine (*Aquilegia canadensis*). An additional companion for more consistently moist areas is wild ginger (*Asarum canadense*), with its bold, heart-shaped leaves to contrast with Pennsylvania sedge's delicate appearance.

DID YOU KNOW?

The specific epithet (or species name) *pensylvanica* is a reference to this plant being "of Pennsylvania." That said, it grows and thrives in most of eastern North America.

Carex plantaginea SEDGE FAMILY (CYPERACEAE)

Seersucker sedge, plantain-leaf sedge

DEER RESISTANCE	HARDINESS ZONES	NORTHEAST NATIVE STATES	HEIGHT/SPREAD
9-10	4-8	CT, MA, MD, ME, NH, NJ, NY, PA, VA, VT, WV	10-15 IN. × 10-15 IN.

Seersucker sedge features $\frac{1}{2}$- to 1-in. wide, semi-evergreen, puckered leaves of pale to medium green, with reddish pigmented bases. These are arranged in robust whorls at ground level. In early spring, it produces 10-in. long stalks of wind-pollinated inflorescences that are considered aesthetically insignificant. These will, however, produce seed, and with the proper conditions, young plants may emerge within a year or two. These can be allowed to thrive in place, or transplanted to other areas of the garden. Seersucker is considered a broadleaf sedge, and is a most attractive foliage plant for its uniquely textured leaves. It thrives in light to medium shade, and is a perfect addition to wildflower and woodland gardens, as a border along walkways, at the base of trees, and almost any other spot where its leaf clusters can be enjoyed.

CULTURE AND TIPS

This sedge is easy to grow in a wide range of soils except for those that are poorly drained and wet, or extremely dry. As a woodland plant, it thrives best in rich, moist soils that are high in organic matter. It grows as a tight clump, or crown, composed of many single plants, and the clumps can easily be divided. Those individual plants can be replanted successfully, even with very few roots, and will readily form new clumps. As with all sedges, water well until established.

Carex plantaginea features broad, puckered leaves.

COMPANION PLANTS

Seersucker sedge is complemented by larger plants and ferns. Northern lady fern (*Athyrium filix-femina*) makes an excellent companion, especially the form with red stems, as does marginal wood fern (*Dryopteris marginalis*). For flowering companions, consider rue-anemone (*Thalictrum thalictroides*), wild bleeding heart (*Dicentra eximia*), and red columbine (*Aquilegia canadensis*).

DID YOU KNOW?

The common name seersucker sedge refers to the fact that its puckered, light green leaves resemble gathered seersucker fabric.

Carex platyphylla SEDGE FAMILY (CYPERACEAE)

Silver sedge, broadleaf sedge

DEER RESISTANCE	HARDINESS ZONES	NORTHEAST NATIVE STATES	HEIGHT/SPREAD
9-10	4-8	CT, MA, MD, ME, NH, NJ, NY, PA, VA, VT, WV	8-10 IN. × 10-15 IN.

Silver sedge features ½- to 1-in. wide, evergreen leaves of pale bluish green arranged in sizable rosettes. It is one of the largest-leaved of the broadleaf sedges, and makes a decided statement with its bold, cool-colored, ridged foliage. It thrives in light to medium shade, and is a welcome color addition to naturalistic gardens, tempering hard edges of walkways, or tucked happily in the root flares of large trees. It deserves a spot where it can be admired.

CULTURE AND TIPS

Silver sedge is easy to grow in rich, moist soils that are high in organic matter. Like other sedges, it grows as a tight clump, or crown, composed of many single plants, that can easily be separated and divided. Single plants can be replanted to form new clumps in a short time. When happy, silver sedge may reseed and spread. Make sure to keep newly transplanted divisions and seedlings well watered until they're established.

Carex platyphylla offers unique, bluish green color, as well as broad, clumping foliage.

A light mulch of finely shredded leaves in fall is beneficial, especially for building moisture-retaining organic matter in the soil.

COMPANION PLANTS

Silver sedge is nicely complemented by other *Carex* species, as well as ferns. The dark green foliage of Christmas fern (*Polystichum acrostichoides*) and vertical fronds of maidenhair fern (*Adiantum pedatum*) add welcome textural interest. For flowering companions, consider green-and-gold (*Chrysogonum virginanum*), nodding onion (*Allium cernuum*), and early meadow rue (*Thalictrum dioicum*).

DID YOU KNOW?

This plant is sometimes commonly called broadleaf sedge. Like other members of this group of sedges, this name refers to the fact that its bluish green leaves are some of the widest in its genus.

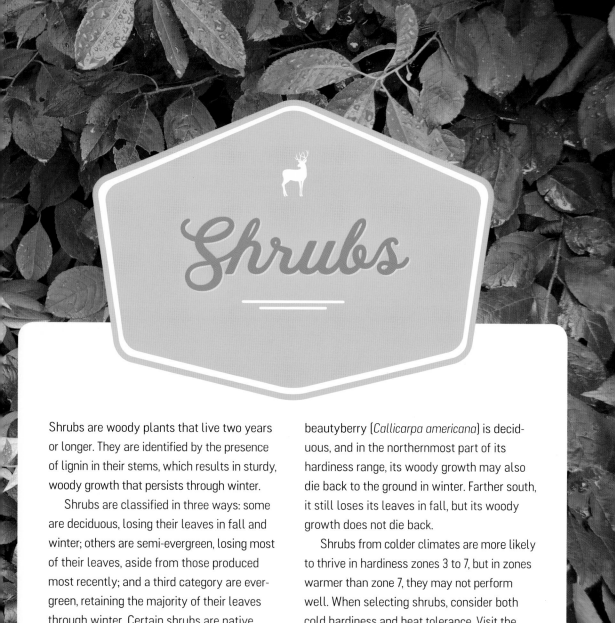

Shrubs

Shrubs are woody plants that live two years or longer. They are identified by the presence of lignin in their stems, which results in sturdy, woody growth that persists through winter.

Shrubs are classified in three ways: some are deciduous, losing their leaves in fall and winter; others are semi-evergreen, losing most of their leaves, aside from those produced most recently; and a third category are evergreen, retaining the majority of their leaves through winter. Certain shrubs are native to and perform well in the Northeast, even though primarily they hail from farther south. These are referred to as "tender," and they perform differently depending upon where they're planted within (or relative to) their native range. For example, American beautyberry (*Callicarpa americana*) is deciduous, and in the northernmost part of its hardiness range, its woody growth may also die back to the ground in winter. Farther south, it still loses its leaves in fall, but its woody growth does not die back.

Shrubs from colder climates are more likely to thrive in hardiness zones 3 to 7, but in zones warmer than zone 7, they may not perform well. When selecting shrubs, consider both cold hardiness and heat tolerance. Visit the USDA Plant Hardiness Zones website to learn more: https://planthardiness.ars.usda.gov

We have selected fifteen native shrubs that we find to be exceptionally useful in the landscape, and in our experience, are seldom browsed by deer.

Amelanchier laevis ROSE FAMILY (ROSACEAE)
Allegheny serviceberry, shadblow

DEER RESISTANCE	HARDINESS ZONES	NORTHEAST NATIVE STATES	HEIGHT/SPREAD
7-9	4-8	CT, DC, DE, MA, ME, NH, NJ, NY, PA, RI, VA, VT, WV	15-25 FT. × 15-25 FT.

This deciduous, multi-stemmed shrub provides four seasons of interest. Its bronzy-purplish spring foliage emerges about the same time as its pendulous, 4- to 5-in. long clusters of white flowers come into bloom. These are five-petaled and fragrant. Though the flowers may only last a week or so before succumbing to early spring weather, the display they produce is outstanding. Purplish black, blueberry-like fruit follows in summer, providing a veritable feast for birds. As fall approaches, the foliage mounts a fiery display of reds, yellows, and oranges. The branch structure and silvery bark of Allegheny serviceberry is especially evident and appreciated in winter.

'Cumulus' (20-25 ft. × 6-8 ft.) and 'Snowcloud' (15-20 ft. × 10-15 ft.), also known as 'Majestic', are narrow, fastigiate forms, good for street trees if kept pruned. 'Spring Flurry' (25-28 ft. × 15-20 ft.) blooms prolifically in spring, and brightens the fall landscape with foliage changing to brilliant orange and red.

Downy serviceberry or juneberry (A. arborea) is another excellent species, similar in size to Allegheny serviceberry, with young foliage that is downy and grayish beneath. White flowers are carried on drooping 2- to 4-in. racemes, followed by sweet, edible, purplish blue fruits. It tolerates urban conditions well, making it valuable as a city tree. Allegheny and downy serviceberries have produced a natural hybrid known as apple serviceberry (A. ×grandiflora). Cultivar 'Autumn Brilliance' (15-25 ft. × 15-25 ft.) is the best known of this hybrid. 'Robin Hill' (20-30 ft. × 12-15 ft.) is pink-flowered.

The best fruit-producing species is Saskatoon serviceberry (A. alnifolia; 10-13 ft. × 8-9 ft.), which has several prolific cultivars—'Obelisk' (12-15 ft. × 3-4 ft.) and 'Regent' (4-6 ft. × 4-6 ft.) are notable.

All are well suited to wildlife and naturalized gardens, woodland edges, and shrub borders. Plant them too as informal hedges and screens.

CULTURE AND TIPS
Find a sunny or part-shaded spot for easy-care Allegheny serviceberry. It thrives in a range of soils, but well-drained loam that remains moist

Amelanchier laevis blooms in spring with white flowers, a perfect foil to purplish emerging foliage.

is ideal. Keep well watered—soil must not dry out unduly in summer heat. Prune tree-form specimens only to remove dead wood. Serviceberry tolerates black walnut trees growing nearby, as they are indifferent to the toxic compound called juglone walnuts produce through their roots. Be on the lookout for fungal diseases such as fire blight, canker, and powdery mildew, which may appear if plants become stressed.

COMPANION PLANTS

Serviceberry is especially appropriate in informal naturalized areas, and grows well with mapleleaf viburnum (*Viburnum acerifolium*) and arrowwood (*Viburnum dentatum*). Red columbine (*Aquilegia canadensis*), Indian pink (*Spigelia marilandica*), and wild bleeding heart (*Dicentra eximia*) are attractive perennial companions.

For foliage combinations, consider Pennsylvania sedge (*Carex pensylvanica*) and spreading sedge (*Carex laxiculmis*).

DID YOU KNOW?

Native Americans were said to have harvested this shrub's edible berries and dried them like raisins. An alternate common name is shadblow, and refers to the time of bloom, when the fish species called shad is running in rivers and streams. Many birds flock to serviceberry as soon as its fruit ripens—cedar waxwings, gray catbirds, mockingbirds, and thrashers are particularly frequent guests. Bees, especially native bumblebees, harvest the nectar the flowers produce, and are essential for pollination and fruit production.

SHRUBS

Aronia arbutifolia ROSE FAMILY (ROSACEAE)

Red chokeberry

DEER RESISTANCE	HARDINESS ZONES	NORTHEAST NATIVE STATES	HEIGHT/SPREAD
7-9	4-9	CT, DC, DE, MA, MD, ME, NH, NJ, NY, PA, RI, VA, VT, WV	6-12 FT. × 3-6 FT.

Red berries in late summer and fall give red chokeberry its common name.

Multi-stemmed and deciduous, this handsome shrub earns its keep year-round, developing thickets of growth that provide good cover for wildlife. Its erect, vase-shaped habit makes quite a statement in late spring, when it's covered with tightly packed clusters of five-petaled, white flowers that bloom on mature wood. These are followed by tart, red, 1/4-in. berries in late summer that persist well into winter, or until they're eaten by birds. Berries that remain after frost are sweeter, and birds are naturally more attracted to them. Red choke-berry's glossy foliage turns bright red in fall, and makes it an excellent substitute for exotic, invasive burning bush (*Euonymus alatus*).

Compact 'Brilliantissima' (6–8 ft. × 3–4 ft.) displays a tighter growth habit and grows more slowly than the species. Larger, abundant, vivid

Aronia arbutifolia is a sensational native shrub year-round.

red berries and improved fall color make this selection popular for residential properties on woodland edges, in rain gardens, as hedges, and naturalized in wildlife gardens.

Black chokeberry [*A. melanocarpa*; 3-6 ft. × 3-6 ft.] is similarly low maintenance, but has butterfly-attracting white flowers and black fruit. This sour fruit is considered anti-viral and anti-bacterial. It is also a colonizer. 'Eastland' [4-6 ft. × 6-8 ft.] is an outstanding cultivar of this species to group in shrub borders and alongside streams and ponds. If space is limited, try compact cultivars such as Iroquois Beauty or 'Morton' [2-3 ft. × 4-5 ft.] as a low hedge, or 'Ground Hog' [8-14 in. × 24-36 in.], whose shorter stature makes it much like a groundcover.

These thrive in full to part sun. Large, purple-fruited chokeberry [*A.* ×*prunifolia*; 8-12 ft. × 6-9 ft.] is a natural hybrid of *A. melanocarpa* and *A. arbutifolia*. 'Viking' [3-6 ft. × 3-6 ft.] and similar 'Autumn Magic' are excellent cultivars of this hybrid.

CULTURE AND TIPS

Aronia prefers to grow in full sun or part shade, on sites where the soil remains moist in summer. It tolerates wet, boggy soils well, and may be used to control erosion. It is not fussy about pH, and also tolerates drought. If pruning is needed, do so immediately after bloom. Remove suckers to control spread as necessary. Pests and diseases are rarely an issue.

Red chokeberry has bright white flowers in spring, a favorite with pollinators. Shown here is cultivar 'Brilliantissima'.

COMPANION PLANTS

Various species of serviceberry (*Amelanchier* spp.) and summersweet (*Clethra alnifolia*) are compatible shrub choices. Northern blue flag (*Iris versicolor*), cardinal flower (*Lobelia cardinalis*), and common sneezeweed (*Helenium autumnale*), make excellent flowering companions.

DID YOU KNOW?

Chokeberry fruit is almost three times as high in antioxidants as wild blueberries. Use it in smoothies, cookies, muffins, pies, and other goodies. Butterflies and bees enjoy nectar from the flowers, and birds are attracted to the nutrient-dense fruits.

Callicarpa americana   MINT FAMILY (LAMIACEAE [LABIATAE])
American beautyberry

DEER RESISTANCE	HARDINESS ZONES	NORTHEAST NATIVE STATES	HEIGHT/SPREAD
8-10	6-10	MD, VA	3-8 FT. × 3-8 FT.

The attraction of American beautyberry as a garden ornamental lies in the long-lasting and showy clusters of bright, magenta-violet fruits that encircle the stems' leaf nodes from late summer to early fall. The small lavender or pink summer flowers, borne on new wood, appear more or less inconsequential to humans, but are valued by bees. In fall, the foliage turns brilliant yellow, in dramatic contrast to the berries. Fruit production is reputed to be best where several plants can cross-pollinate, although each is self-fertile.

Quick to establish, American beautyberry is an easy-care deciduous shrub that produces a good display the first year of planting, and offers good winter cover for wildlife. When grouped in a sunny spot, plants bring height and late interest to the back of shrub borders. They are fine additions to rain gardens and woodland edges, wildlife gardens, along fences, in mass plantings, and are even effective as specimen or container plants. 'Lactea' is a form that has white berries.

CULTURE AND TIPS

American beautyberry thrives in sunny or partly shaded spots in the garden. Soil should drain well, although it need not be rich; very poor soils can be amended with organic matter to improve fertility, making fertilizer unnecessary. Although it's considered drought-tolerant, beautyberry should not be allowed to dry out thoroughly. Increase by seed, or transplant volunteers that may germinate at the base of the plants. Softwood cuttings usually root easily, and pests and diseases are seldom a problem. Beautyberry flowers on new wood, so be sure to prune back to 12 in. from the ground in early spring, before bud break, to encourage vigorous new growth and better berry production later in the season.

SHRUBS

Fruit of *Callicarpa americana* is an especially showy addition to the fall garden.

COMPANION PLANTS

New York ironweed (*Vernonia noveboracensis*), especially the cultivar 'Summer's Swan Song', as well as beebalm (*Monarda* spp.) and Maryland senna (*Senna marilandica*) are good perennial additions. Shrubby St. John's wort (*Hypericum prolificum*) and mapleleaf viburnum (*Viburum acerifolium*) are two useful shrub companions.

DID YOU KNOW?

Technically, the astringent berries of this shrub are edible, but so bitter they're barely palatable when raw; once cooked, however, they can be made into jam and wine. Finches, cardinals, woodpeckers, and other birds feed on the berries in fall. Research has shown that compounds in the fresh leaves of American beautyberry are effective in repelling ticks, flies, gnats, and mosquitoes, as well as other biting insects.

Calycanthus floridus CAROLINA ALLSPICE FAMILY (CALYCANTHACEAE)

Carolina allspice, sweetshrub

DEER RESISTANCE	HARDINESS ZONES	NORTHEAST NATIVE STATES	HEIGHT/SPREAD
9-10	4-9	CT, DC, DE, MA, MD, NY, PA, VA, WV	6-10 FT. × 6-12 FT.

This deciduous understory shrub is found in the wild mostly in shady woodlands, often alongside rivers and streams. In late spring, fragrant, reddish brown, 2-in. flowers open at the ends of short, hairy twigs over several weeks. The unusual, upright blooms are followed by brown, drooping, urn-shaped seed capsules, some 3 to 4 in. long. These contain several large seeds, and persist through winter. Pairs of shiny 6-in. leaves turn golden in fall. When wounded or bruised, twigs and foliage emit a pleasant aroma, hence the common name.

Several cultivars and hybrids are on the market, including 'Burgundy Spice' (6-8 ft. × 6-8 ft.), with dark purple leaves and wine-red flowers in spring, and 'Athens' (5-7 ft. × 5-7 ft.), which sports especially fragrant yellow flowers. Hybrids, such as relatively dwarf 'Aphrodite' (4-7 ft. × 4-7 ft.), with its rich red blooms, delight all summer. The flowers of 'Hartlage Wine' (6-8 ft. × 6-8 ft.) are a bit smaller and less intensely red. In late spring, sterile 'Venus' (5-7 ft. × 5-7 ft.) produces 4-in. white flowers accented with central purple and yellow markings, resembling those of star magnolia (*Magnolia stellata*). California sweetshrub, (*C. occidentalis*) is a western native species.

Carolina allspice is valuable in containers, cutting gardens, and as a specimen plant, as well as in woodlands, ornamental shrub borders, foundation plantings, and screening hedges.

CULTURE AND TIPS

This low-maintenance shrub does best in full sun to part shade. It is not fussy about soil, whether clay or wet, but enjoys a rich, well-drained loam when available. Propagate from seed in springtime, softwood cuttings in summer, or by dividing the rootstock. Although it self-sows, this plant is not invasive—it does, however, tend to colonize by suckers, and these can be removed if necessary. Prune as needed after bloom time. It is wise to buy plants when they are in bloom, because individual plants differ widely in the intensity of their flowers' fragrance. Fortunately, all are resistant to pests and diseases.

SHRUBS

Calycanthus floridus features red flowers that often smell like fruit, and the foliage and stems, when crushed, have a spicy aroma.

COMPANION PLANTS

Shrub partners could include red-osier dogwood (*Cornus sericea*) and red chokeberry (*Aronia arbutifolia*). Biennial purple phacelia (*Phacelia bipinnatifida*) along with perennial yellow star tickseed (*Coreopsis pubescens*) make attractive companions.

DID YOU KNOW?

An essential oil is distilled from the flowers of Carolina allspice for use in high quality perfumes, and its dried leaves are sometimes added to potpourri. Fruit flies and sap beetles are its main pollinators, no doubt attracted to the fruity aroma of the flowers.

Ceanothus americanus BUCKTHORN FAMILY (RHAMNACEAE)

New Jersey tea, redroot

DEER RESISTANCE	HARDINESS ZONES	NORTHEAST NATIVE STATES	HEIGHT/SPREAD
7-9	3-8	CT, DC, DE, MA, MD, NY, PA, VA, WV	3-4 FT. × 3-5 FT.

New Jersey tea has attractive clusters of flowers in late spring and early summer.

Deciduous New Jersey tea is a low-growing, dense, mounding shrub. Its deep, strong taproots make it exceedingly useful as a large-scale groundcover, especially to stabilize soil on banks and hillsides. In late spring, loose clusters of white, four- or five-parted, 1/4-in. flowers bloom at stem tips and in leaf axils. Good for cutting, the flowers are quite fragrant, and many bees, butterflies, and other insects visit regularly. Pairs of glossy, oval leaves, rimmed with teeth, are medium green, but gray with hairs beneath. New Jersey tea is excellent as a drought-tolerant hedge, and is appropriate for native plant gardens and shrub borders.

CULTURE AND TIPS

New Jersey tea thrives in sunny or partly shaded sites, as well as slightly deeper shade. Average, well-drained soils are fine, as are

SHRUBS

sandy or rocky ones, and even limestone-based soils with a higher pH. This plant tolerates difficult planting positions, including under black walnut trees. Mulch young plants routinely with compost or other organic matter to encourage deep rooting. Established plants are difficult to move or transplant due to their tough taproots. There is seldom a need to prune New Jersey tea, as it remains compact when untended. Plants are sometimes susceptible to powdery mildew and leaf spot, but generally pest and disease free.

COMPANION PLANTS

Many showy perennials combine well with New Jersey tea, especially butterfly flower (*Asclepias tuberosa*), cultivars of beardtongue (*Penstemon digitalis*) like 'Husker Red', and New York ironweed (*Vernonia noveboracensis*). Underplant with spreading sedge (*Carex laxiculmis*), particularly the cultivar Bunny Blue, for an interesting foliar contrast.

DID YOU KNOW?

During the Revolutionary war, the red roots of this plant were made into "redroot tea," a substitute for banned imported black tea. Both its roots and leaves were once a common remedy for asthma, whooping cough, and bronchitis. Many pollinating insects visit the flowers frequently, but butterflies are its primary pollinators. This plant is a larval host for spring and summer azure butterflies, as well as mottled duskywings. Seed provides food for songbirds, and hummingbirds feed on insect pollinators.

Ceanothus americanus packs a beautiful display into a small shrub.

Clethra alnifolia WHITE ALDER FAMILY (CLETHRACEAE)

Summersweet, sweet pepperbush

DEER RESISTANCE	HARDINESS ZONES	NORTHEAST NATIVE STATES	HEIGHT/SPREAD
8-10	3-9	CT, DE, MA, MD, ME, NH, NJ, NY, PA, RI, VA	3-8 FT. × 4-6 FT.

Summersweet may be found in the wild on sites where soil is wet, such as marshes, beside streams and creeks, and even along shorelines. This deciduous, upright but rounded shrub suckers readily, and left alone, will form substantial colonies. Its many branching stems are clothed in alternate, oval, toothed leaves that turn a showy golden color in autumn. In midsummer, fragrant white flowers (sometimes pink) bloom on new wood in eye-catching, bottlebrush-like, 3- to 8-in. spikes. After the attractive flowers are spent, spikes of seed capsules persist, often through winter and beyond. These pods are not considered aesthetically important, but receive frequent visits from songbirds for seed.

Several fine cultivars of summersweet are in the marketplace. The best known is probably 'Hummingbird' (2-4 ft. × 3-5 ft.), a compact form that has spikes of white flowers, especially appropriate in gardens where space is limited. 'Sixteen Candles' (4-5 ft. × 2-3 ft.) is also relatively compact, and tolerates shade. Its candle-shaped flowers are creamy white. 'Pink Spires' (3-8 ft. × 4-6 ft.) and the rosy-flowered 'Ruby Spice' (4-6 ft. × 3-5 ft.) are both pink-flowered, as their names suggest, and the latter has the deepest pink flowers of any selection. The foliage of white-flowered 'Creel's Calico' (3-4 ft. × 5-6 ft.) is irregularly splashed with white during spring and summer. A southern species, mountain pepperbush (*C. acuminata*), is very similar to *C. alnifolia*, but has pointed leaves.

Summersweet thrives in coastal and rain gardens, beside ponds and streams, and in naturalistic gardens where soil remains damp. It excels in shrub borders, and tolerates shade, but best flowering is achieved in full sun.

[top] *Clethra alnifolia* is a fine native shrub at home in average to wet soils. [above] Summersweet is aptly named for its attractive, fragrant flower clusters in summer.

Pay special attention to where it's sited within the garden, so its heady fragrance can be savored. It can also be used as an informal flowering hedge.

CULTURE AND TIPS

Plant summersweet in average to wet soils in sunny to partly shaded sites. It tolerates salt spray along the coast. If necessary, prune in late winter, as flowers are carried on new wood made the current season. Propagate by stem cuttings taken in early summer. Cuttings of more mature wood can also be taken later; these root better with the use of rooting hormone. Harvested seed can be sown in fall or the following spring. Pests and diseases are seldom a problem.

COMPANION PLANTS

Perennials such as purple coneflower (*Echinacea purpurea*) and its many cultivars); sweet Joe-Pye weed (*Eutrochium purpureum*); cardinal flower (*Lobelia cardinalis*); and great blue lobelia (*Lobelia siphilitica*) are striking companion plants.

DID YOU KNOW?

Pollinators—including many butterfly species, bumblebees, honeybees, and wasps—flock to the fragrant flowers of summersweet. Songbirds visit for nectar, and seed is a valuable source of food when it is scarce in fall and winter. In 2015, *Clethra alnifolia* was named the wildflower of the year by the Virginia Native Plant Society.

Cornus sericea DOGWOOD FAMILY (CORNACEAE)
Red-osier dogwood, red twig dogwood

DEER RESISTANCE	HARDINESS ZONES	NORTHEAST NATIVE STATES	HEIGHT/SPREAD
7-9	3-7	CT, DE, MA, MD, ME, NH, NJ, NY, PA, RI, VA	8-10 FT. × 10-12 FT.

Fast-growing and multi-stemmed, this deciduous, arching shrub provides four-season interest in the garden. Well known and especially appreciated in winter for its young, bright red stems, red-osier dogwood also produces showy, flat-topped, 1- to 2-in. wide clusters of small, white flowers from late spring to early summer.

Cornus sericea is a durable, easy-to-grow shrub with multi-season interest.

Ornamental, bluish white berries on short red stems (called pedicels) follow, and encourage birds to visit. Opposite, oval leaves in medium to dark green turn distinctive shades of purplish red in fall, and later drop to reveal the vibrant red young stems. Stems grown in previous years will be a dull purplish gray. This fibrous-rooted shrub colonizes by suckers; remove unwanted suckers at root level.

Several cultivars worth seeking out are available. Especially popular is red-stemmed 'Cardinal' (8-10 ft. × 8-10 ft.), with outstanding winter stems and a more relaxed habit than the species. Compact Arctic Fire or 'Farrow' (3-5 ft. × 3-5 ft.) is ideal for planting as a specimen in containers. 'Sunshine' (6-10 ft. × 6-10 ft.) has yellowish or chartreuse foliage, sometimes variegated with green, which contrasts well with its red summer stems. 'Flaviramea' (5-8 f.t × 5-8 ft.), known as golden twig dogwood, sports young stems of bright yellow; similar 'Bud's

Yellow' may be somewhat smaller. 'Silver and Gold' (5–7 ft. × 6–8 ft.), a sport of 'Flaviramea' introduced by the Mt. Cuba Center in Delaware, displays attractive, irregularly cream-rimmed foliage that turns yellow in fall. Dwarf 'Neil Z' (3–4 ft. × 3–4 ft.) is commonly known as Pucker-Up because of its lustrous wrinkled or puckered leaves and red stems.

Red-osier dogwood is excellent for massing in the landscape, for hedging and screening, as a specimen plant, or in mixed borders with perennials, annuals, and bulbs. This shrub is an important addition to bird and wildlife gardens, as well as rain gardens.

CULTURE AND TIPS

Red-osier dogwood does well in most soils, including sand and clay, but especially those rich in organic matter that remain wet. Poorly drained, acidic, and alkaline soils are tolerated. Provide a full sun to partly shaded spot in the garden. Encourage dramatic winter stem color by cutting ½ to ⅓ of the older stems to the ground each winter. Otherwise plants can be stooled—that is, cut all stems to about 12 in. from the ground in early spring—to stimulate new stem growth. Propagate by seed, stratified for 60 to 90 days at 41°F. Hardwood cuttings set out in winter root readily. Be alert for dogwood sawfly larvae that can defoliate infested plants, though their leaves will regrow. Leaf blight and canker can also be issues, and should be treated accordingly. Leaf miners sometimes attack young foliage.

COMPANION PLANTS

Summersweet (*Clethra alnifolia*) and winter-berry (*Ilex verticillata*) are excellent companion shrubs for red-osier dogwood. Cardinal flower (*Lobelia cardinalis*), swamp milkweed (*Asclepias incarnata*), and northern blue flag (*Iris versicolor*) all enjoy similar conditions, and add pops of color to the garden in late spring and summer.

DID YOU KNOW?

A large number of bird species visit red-osier dogwood for its berries and for cover, including catbirds, woodpeckers, flickers, and tanagers. It is a larval host for spring azure butterflies. Cut stems make a lively addition to winter containers.

Red-osier dogwood's best feature is its colorful winter stems.

Eubotrys racemosus HEATH FAMILY (ERICACEAE)

Fetterbush, sweetbells leucothoe

DEER RESISTANCE	HARDINESS ZONES	NORTHEAST NATIVE STATES	HEIGHT/SPREAD
7-9	5-9	CT, DC, DE, MA, MD, NJ, NY, PA, RI, VA	4-6 FT. × 4-6 FT.

Fetterbush is an excellent suckering shrub for naturalizing in woodlands where soil remains consistently moist to wet. In spring to early summer, 2- to 4-in. long racemes of ½-in. wide flowers grow from the upper leaf axils. The white or pink-tinged blooms (reminiscent of those of related *Erica*) are pendulous, bell- or urn-shaped, and carried on short stems. Coppery-brown seed capsules follow. Deciduous, pointed, 1- to 3-in. leaves, shallowly rimmed with teeth, are arranged alternately on the stems. Foliage is slightly glossy, and turns shades of golden yellow, orange, and red in fall. In mild climates, it may be semi-evergreen.

If soil conditions allow, fetterbush is valuable in foundation plantings, where it can be protected from windy conditions. The colonizing roots help to prevent soil erosion on slopes and banks, as well as at pond and stream edges. Due to its tendency to colonize, fetterbush can be used as a dense, tall groundcover. It is also referred to as *Leucothoe racemosa*.

CULTURE AND TIPS

This understory woodland shrub demands moist soils that do not dry out in summer. It's best in partly or even fully shaded positions where soil is acidic. Keep away from windy spots where foliage may desiccate, and apply protective winter mulch in cold climates. Rejuvenate plants by removing old stems to the ground as growth commences in spring. Propagate by softwood cuttings in early summer, or take hardwood cuttings in winter. Divide large plants in spring. Leaf spot and root rot may sometimes be problems.

COMPANION PLANTS

Virginia sweetspire (*Itea virginica*), winterberry (*Ilex verticillata*), and red chokeberry (*Aronia arbutifolia*) are appropriate companion shrubs for fetterbush. Combine with blue mistflower (*Conoclinium coelestinum*), New York ironweed, (*Vernonia noveboracensis*), and cardinal flower (*Lobelia cardinalis*) to add flower color.

Eubotrys racemosus makes a great garden shrub featured singly or en masse.

DID YOU KNOW?

The name fetterbush refers to this plant's habit of forming dense thickets that fetter, or impede, progress through the woods. It is closely related to Japanese andromeda (*Pieris japonica*). At bloom time, this plant attracts bees and butter-flies to the garden.

Hypericum prolificum ST. JOHN'S WORT FAMILY (HYPERICACEAE)
Shrubby St. John's wort

DEER RESISTANCE	HARDINESS ZONES	NORTHEAST NATIVE STATES	HEIGHT/SPREAD
8-9	3-8	CT, DC, DE, MA, MD, ME, NJ, NY, PA, RI, VA, VT, WV	1-4 FT. × 1-4 FT.

Shrubby St. John's wort is well named for its dense, bushy growth. This small to medium, rounded, deciduous shrub has an upright habit. Its slender, 2- to 3-in. long, bright green to bluish leaves are arranged in opposite pairs. When the young green stems mature, they become woody and light brown, and outer bark exfoliates in winter to reveal attractive orange-bronze inner bark. Brilliant, buttercup yellow blooms cover

The bright, cheery yellow flowers of shrubby St. John's wort adorn the shrub from June through August.

the shrubs from early to midsummer. Clusters of four to seven flowers are borne in leaf axils and at stem tips. The five-petaled blooms, each 1 in. or so wide, are highlighted with a central mass of long, pollen-laden stamens. Pointed, oval seed capsules follow, persist into winter, and split at maturity to release abundant seeds. Fall color is minimal.

Dense or bushy St. John's wort (*H. densiflorum*; 4-6 ft. × 3-4 ft.) is another fine-textured shrub, with densely twiggy stems. It is similar to shrubby St. John's wort, but has larger, nearly flat-topped clusters of ½-in. wide flowers all summer, and promises yellow-green fall color. The 1-in. wide flowers of 'Buttercup' (2-3 ft. × 2-3 ft.) are slightly fragrant, and continue well into fall. 'Creel's Gold Star' (3-5 ft. × 3-5 ft.) flowers similarly in summer.

Few pests and diseases attack shrubby St. John's wort. This underused, low to medium shrub is effective in mixed woody borders, native rock gardens, along pathways, or in foundation plantings, and can also be cut for dried winter bouquets.

Hypericum prolificum is a relatively small shrub effective en masse as a hedge, or tucked singly into a perennial border.

CULTURE AND TIPS

Shrubby St. John's wort is very forgiving about growing conditions. It does best in full sun or light to part shade, in average well-drained soils; however, dry, sandy, and rocky soils are acceptable, as is occasional flooding. This plant also tolerates alkaline soils, and the salty conditions of seashore gardens, as well as the difficult growing conditions under black walnut trees. Prune in early spring if needed. Start from seeds in fall—be sure to leave seeds uncovered—or root softwood cuttings taken in early summer.

COMPANION PLANTS

New Jersey tea (*Ceanothus americanus*) is a fine shrub companion, along with perennials such as black-eyed Susan (*Rudbeckia hirta*) and prairie rosinweed (*Silphium terebinthinaceum*). Switchgrass (*Panicum virginicum*), and especially its blue-hued cultivars 'Dallas Blues' and 'Thundercloud', combines well with shrubby St. John's wort.

DID YOU KNOW?

The species name refers to the abundance of stamens each flower produces. Native bumblebees are the primary pollinators, and throng the plants during bloom time to harvest nectar and pollen. Gray hairstreak butterflies lay their eggs on shrubby St. John's wort to feed emerging caterpillars.

Ilex verticillata HOLLY FAMILY (AQUIFOLIACEAE)

Winterberry, black alder

DEER RESISTANCE	HARDINESS ZONES	NORTHEAST NATIVE STATES	HEIGHT/SPREAD
9-10	3-9	CT, DC, DE, MA, MD, ME, NH, NJ, NY, PA, RI, VA, VT, WV	6-15 FT. × 6-15 FT.

Winterberry's common name comes from brightly colored berries that last for months, and provide birds with winter sustenance.

To catch sight of a fully fruited specimen of winterberry on a fall or early winter hike is always a joy. Most of us think of hollies as evergreens, but winterberry drops it leaves in fall to reveal smooth, pale brown branches, often laden with ¼-in. bright red berries. These persist into winter until they ripen and are either devoured by birds or drop to the ground. Multi-stemmed winterberry has an upright habit, and in damp to wet soils where it grows well, it often colonizes into thickets. Dark green leaves, rimmed with small teeth, are arranged alternately on the stem. Fall color is understated, as are small, white, inconspicuous flowers, which appear in late spring on separate male and female plants (termed dioecious), but these are sought after by bumblebees. Both sexes are necessary for pollination and the berry production that results—it is recommended to plant one male for every three to five females.

Ilex verticillata is one of our finest native shrubs for deer resistance and garden worthiness.

Many cultivars and hybrids are on the market, but it is advisable to select males and females that bloom at the same time for best fruit production. Many feature reddish orange and yellow berries, as well as red. Early-blooming cultivars include 'Afterglow', 'Stop-light', 'Red Sprite', and 'Cacapon'; male 'Jim Dandy' is the favorite pollinator to plant nearby. 'Southern Gentleman' is the popular male for later-blooming 'Winter Red', 'Scarlett O'Hara', yellow-berried 'Winter Gold', and the hybrid 'Sparkleberry' (*I. verticillata* ×*I. serrata*). 'Apollo' and long-blooming 'Raritan Chief' are also good pollinators for the hybrids. All are excellent in rain gardens, in shrub and mixed borders, and in low, wet areas beside streams and ponds. They are good informal hedges as well.

Inkberry or gallberry (*I. glabra*; 5–9 ft. × 5–9 ft.) is a species of broadleaf evergreen holly grown for its foliage. It is a medium-textured shrub that also forms colonies or thickets, especially in wet places, which it prefers. When pollinated, the female plant produces pea-sized black berries that are aesthetically insignificant, but enjoyed by birds. Bees that feed on inkberry flowers produce prized gallberry honey.

CULTURE AND TIPS

Winterberry does well in sun or part shade in medium to wet soil high in organic matter, and it tolerates poor drainage well. Soil pH must be acidic for this shrub to thrive. Berry production is said to be more abundant in sunny places, and in the wild, it is found alongside streams and creeks. Harvesting berried branches for use in holiday arrangements and containers is popular, and if you do choose to do so, take the opportunity to prune your shrub for better form and structure. Propagation is best by taking cuttings in early summer. Powdery mildew and leaf spot are occasional problems.

COMPANION PLANTS

Be sure to plant a male pollinator near female winterberries. The red winter stems of moisture-loving red-osier dogwood (*Cornus sericea*)

provide a cheerful color echo to winterberry's red fruits. Plant ostrich fern (*Matteuccia struthiopteris*) as a dramatic groundcover. Moisture-loving companion perennials include blue mistflower (*Conoclinium coelestinum*), cardinal flower (*Lobelia cardinalis*), and swamp milkweed (*Asclepias incarnata*).

DID YOU KNOW?

Eastern bluebirds, American robins, and cedar waxwings are among the most frequent birds that feed on this shrub's berries, and can often be observed harvesting fruit from branches used in holiday containers. Dense thickets of winterberry also provide excellent nesting sites for many bird species.

Itea virginica SWEETSPIRE FAMILY (ITEACEAE)

Virginia sweetspire, tassel-white

DEER RESISTANCE	HARDINESS ZONES	NORTHEAST NATIVE STATES	HEIGHT/SPREAD
6-8	5-9	DC, DE, MD, NJ, PA, VA	3-5 FT. × 4-6 FT.

Sweetly scented spikes of white flowers adorn Virginia sweetspire in spring, to the delight of gardeners and pollinators alike.

This deciduous, mounded, slowly spreading shrub is best known for two things: its showy, 2- to 6-in. spikes of deliciously fragrant white flowers in late spring to early summer and its brilliantly multicolored fall foliage. Virginia sweetspire's 4-in. leaves (dark green, oblong, and edged irregularly with tiny teeth) are borne alternately on its stems. Fall color is quite dramatic and can persist over several weeks depending on weather, with foliage turning reddish purple, crimson, and sometimes even fluorescent red. With maturity, Virginia sweetspire becomes densely branched, especially toward the tops of the stems, giving a somewhat crowded effect that can be useful for screening. Because it spreads by runners, this shrub can form dense thickets, an especially desirable trait any place masses are encouraged.

Some popular cultivars are available, including 'Henry's Garnet' (3-4 ft. × 4-6 ft.), a dwarf form called 'Little Henry' (1½-2 ft. × 2-2½ ft.), and 'Saturnalia' (3–4 ft. × 4–5 ft.), which blooms slightly earlier than the others. Compact 'Scentlandia' (2–3 ft. × 2–3 ft.) boasts improved hardiness.

Sweetspire is valuable in sunny rain gardens as well as damp, shaded locations in woodlands, along stream banks, as well as sites with average soils. It can be used to create effective foundation plantings, shrub borders, and for naturalizing in wild or native plant gardens.

CULTURE AND TIPS

Easy-to-grow Virginia sweetspire tolerates shade, but is at its best in full sun. While it accepts wet soil and occasional flooding, this shrub thrives in well-drained soil high in organic matter that doesn't dry out. Retain soil moisture and lessen temperature fluctuations by applying an organic mulch in spring. Sweetspire tolerates dry conditions once it's well established. Flowers are carried on old wood made the previous year, so prune to shape or control size right after bloom time. Pests and diseases are seldom a problem, though mildew and leaf spot may attack when plants are stressed. Increase by taking softwood cuttings 6 to 8 in. long in spring, or semi-hardwood cuttings in late summer and early fall. Seed collected in fall and refrigerated through winter should be sown the following spring. If solitary or tightly clumped shrubs are your preference, an annual trim of spreading rootstocks just below ground level, at the shrub's base, is enough to discourage spreading.

COMPANION PLANTS

Highlight Virginia sweetspire's late summer and fall foliage display by combining it with perennials, including Hubricht's bluestar (*Amsonia hubrichtii*), spotted Joe-Pye weed (*Eutrochium maculatum*), and tall ironweed (*Vernonia angustifolia*). Red-osier dogwood (*Cornus sericea*) and northern bayberry (*Morella pensylvanica*) make attractive shrub companions.

DID YOU KNOW?

Virginia sweetspire's conspicuous, fragrant flowers attract nectar-loving sweat bees and native bumblebees. It provides good cover and habitat for birds, and is a host plant for holly azure butterfly caterpillars. In the wild, it's found in freshwater wetlands, but it adapts very well to regular garden situations, and has become well utilized in the landscape trade.

Itea virginica grows wild in bogs and marshes, but it's perfectly at home in the typical garden. Shown here is 'Henry's Garnet'.

Lindera benzoin LAUREL FAMILY (LAURACEAE)

Spicebush, wild allspice

DEER RESISTANCE
9-10

HARDINESS ZONES
4-9

NORTHEAST NATIVE STATES
CT, DC, DE, MA, MD, ME, NH, NJ, NY, PA, RI, VA, VT, WV

HEIGHT/SPREAD
6-12 FT. × 6-12 FT.

Spicebush is a deciduous understory plant that has an uncluttered, graceful vase shape. It is dioecious, with separate male and female plants. Fragrant, greenish yellow flowers are tiny, and cluster at the leaf nodes early in spring,

Vase-shaped *Lindera benzoin* blooms with tiny yellow flowers in spring.

before other trees have leafed out. The male flowers are showier because they're comprised of soft stamens. Greenish, ½-in. berries ripen to yellow and then bright red, and are borne on female plants that have been pollinated. Stems are slender, with grayish brown or olive-colored bark; scratch the stem and you can smell the wonderfully spicy fragrance, hence the common name. Thick leaves, each about 6 in. long, are borne alternately on stems, and are also fragrant when crushed. Foliage turns a vibrant yellow in fall, before leaf drop. It is wise to group several male and female plants together to insure fruit production.

Spicebush shrubs are excellent for damp native plant gardens, massed on the edge of moist woodlands, and in shrub borders, especially in shade.

CULTURE AND TIPS

Provide sun, part sun, or even light shade for spicebush. Best berry production and fall color occur in lightly shaded spots. It does best in moist, acidic soils, so it's advisable to maintain

Female plants of spicebush bear fruit that ripens to bright red.

soil moisture and stable soil temperatures by mulching with shredded leaves. Pruning is seldom necessary; pests and diseases are few. Plants can be grown from seed, best collected as fruits redden. Remove the flesh and sow at once to overwinter cold and germinate the following spring. Softwood cuttings may be taken from midsummer on, and root more readily with the use of rooting hormone.

COMPANION PLANTS

Consider planting purple-fruited American beautyberry (*Callicarpa americana*) as a foil for golden-leaved spicebush in fall. In light woodlands, evergreen Christmas fern (*Polystichum acrostichoides*) is a compatible ground cover. To add flower color in sunnier situations, try great blue lobelia (*Lobelia siphilitica*) and deep lavender mistflower (*Conoclinium coelestinum*).

DID YOU KNOW?

Spicebush is a friend to many species of wildlife, and is a host plant for spicebush swallowtail butterflies. When they hatch, the caterpillars build unusual nests for protection, and take on a snakelike camouflage. Wood thrushes are especially fond of lipid-rich spicebush berries, although many other bird species visit often, including eastern kingbirds, catbirds, American robins, and white-throated sparrows. Spicebush tea was made from leaves and young twigs during the Civil War, when coffee and black tea were scarce. Dried berries taste spicy, and may be used to perk up apple pies and cobblers.

Morella pensylvanica BAYBERRY FAMILY (MYRICACEAE)

Northern bayberry

DEER RESISTANCE	HARDINESS ZONES	NORTHEAST NATIVE STATES	HEIGHT/SPREAD
9-10	3-7	CT, DC, DE, MA, MD, ME, NH, NJ, NY, PA, RI, VA, VT, WV	5-10 FT. × 3-10 FT.

The multiple branches of northern bayberry result in dense, mounded shrubs that spread by underground rhizomes. These may form colonies that control erosion very effectively, especially on sand dunes, shaded banks, and sites where soil is prone to erosion. In most areas, the foliage is evergreen, but the plant becomes semi-evergreen in its northernmost range. In mid-spring, insignificant, greenish yellow flowers appear on separate male and female plants. Pollen from the green male catkin flowers is disseminated by wind; pollinated female flowers produce clusters of small white berries covered with gray, aromatic wax. These berries persist until consumed by birds, and provide interest in the garden during winter months. Alternate, egg-shaped, lustrous leaves are gray-green and leathery, about 4 in. long. The surface is dotted with resin glands that emit a delightful aroma. Northern bayberry also goes by the botanical name *Myrica pensylvanica*.

An evergreen southern counterpart of this plant, southern bayberry or wax myrtle (*M. cerifera*; 10-15 ft. × 8-10 ft.), is taller and very fast growing. It makes an excellent beach plant for controlling dune erosion, and is hardy in zones 7 to 10. Plant the female cultivar 'Don's Dwarf' (3-5 ft. × 3-5 ft.) and male 'Tom's Dwarf' (3-4 ft. × 4-6 ft.) near each other to ensure good berry production. Both are resistant to leaf spot that may attack the foliage.

Bayberry is appropriate for rain gardens, informal screens, and hedges, as well as shrub and mixed borders, especially in coastal gardens requiring salt-tolerant plants. Use it to hold steep banks and in locations where soils can range from wet to dry.

Morella pensylvanica is a hardy evergreen shrub that adapts well to many sites, including coastal areas.

CULTURE AND TIPS

Plant low-maintenance northern bayberry in full sun to part shade. It is not fussy about soil, and does well in acidic or alkaline clay, loamy or sandy soils, and even those that drain poorly. It tolerates lean soils, drought, and salt well, even road salt, where it is used to control ice and snow. Prune to remove dead or damaged wood, or to shape, in early spring. Increase by means of semi-hardwood cuttings; rooting hormone powder aids this process. Sow seed in fall, and overwinter outdoors for germination the following spring.

Northern bayberry has fragrant stems, foliage, and berries.

COMPANION PLANTS

Partner bayberry with other shrubs like inkberry (*Ilex glabra*), New Jersey tea (*Ceanothus americanus*), and winterberry (*Ilex verticillata*). In drier conditions, plant with blanket flower (*Gaillardia pulchella*), black-eyed Susan (*Rudbeckia hirta*), and star tickseed (*Coreopsis pubescens*). Ornamental grasses are also fitting companions, including switchgrass (*Panicum virgatum*) and prairie dropseed (*Sporobolus heterolepis*).

DID YOU KNOW?

Bayberry candles are made from the aromatic wax that coats the berries. Tree swallows, catbirds, and others flock to harvest the valuable berries for food in fall and winter, and are the primary means of seed distribution. The seeds' waxy coating is removed in the gut of the birds. Birds also rely on the shrubs for shelter and cover in exposed areas. Northern bayberry is a host plant for Columbia silk moths, which lay their eggs on its foliage. Some chefs use the dried berries and young foliage to add a unique flavor to stews and sauces.

Osmanthus americanus OLIVE FAMILY (OLEACEAE)
Devilwood, wild olive

DEER RESISTANCE	HARDINESS ZONES	NORTHEAST NATIVE STATES	HEIGHT/SPREAD
9-10	5-9	VA	15-25 FT. × 15-25 FT.

Found in the wild along streams and in swampy areas, in its native range, evergreen devilwood develops slowly into a small, rounded, vase-shaped tree. North of that, which includes most of the Northeast, it grows as a multi-branched shrub of comparatively modest stature.

Osmanthus americanus is a highly adaptable, native evergreen that adapts to shade, drought, and salt.

Relatively rare in the trade, it's known particularly for its attractive, creamy white flowers, blue fruits that attract wildlife, and rich olive-green foliage. Clusters of small, four-lobed flowers appear on stems made in previous years in spring, urn-shaped and highly fragrant. Oval, wavy-edged, 4- to 8-in. long leaves are leathery, and decorate the stems in pairs. Following the flowers, dark blue, olive-like fruit develop, each enclosing a single seed. These remain on the shrub until spring unless consumed by wildlife.

Devilwood tolerates hard pruning well, and may be used as a formal hedge, for screening, naturalizing, or in borders with other shrubs. Its salt tolerance makes it excellent for coastal gardens, or in areas where salt is applied to melt ice in winter.

CULTURE AND TIPS
Devilwood thrives in full sun to partial shade where soil is well drained. Otherwise, it is

SHRUBS

Devilwood blooms with fragrant flowers in spring.

unfussy about soil conditions, and accepts clay, loam, or sand, as long as soil is acidic. Although it prefers consistent moisture, occasional flooding is also tolerated, and when established, the plant is moderately drought tolerant. Pests and diseases are seldom a problem. Prune out dead and thin branches as needed, just after flowering.

COMPANION PLANTS

Partner devilwood with northern bayberry (*Morella pensylvanica*) in seaside gardens, perhaps with red-osier dogwood (*Cornus sericea*). Christmas fern (*Polystichum acrostichoides*) and marginal wood fern (*Dryopteris marginalis*), along with early meadow-rue (*Thalictrum dioicum*) and Indian pink (*Spigelia marilandica*), are especially appropriate in woodland settings.

DID YOU KNOW?

Devilwood is valuable for wildlife in providing cover, and its fruit provides food for birds, squirrels, and other small mammals. Its wood is fine-textured and very strong.

Viburnum dentatum HONEYSUCKLE FAMILY (CAPRIFOLIACEAE)
Arrowwood, southern arrowwood

DEER RESISTANCE	HARDINESS ZONES	NORTHEAST NATIVE STATES	HEIGHT/SPREAD
8-10	2-8	CT, DC, DE, MA, MD, ME, NH, NJ, NY, PA, RI, VA, VT, WV	6-10 FT. × 6-15 FT.

Arrowwood is a dependable, utilitarian shrub with a loosely rounded shape formed by numerous upright, branching stems. It suckers freely from the base, and develops into thickets or loose colonies. Deciduous, opposite leaves are elliptical in shape, and rimmed with wide teeth, hence the species name *dentatum*. Fall color is spotty according to location, with leaves turning

Viburnum dentatum is an easy-to-grow native shrub for sun or shade.

from medium green to light yellow, orange, or pale to deep wine. From late spring into early summer, numerous small white flowers bloom in eye-catching, flat-topped clusters, up to 4 in. across. The flowers are unscented. Round, pea-like berries turn deep blue to purple-black when ripe, and attract countless birds, but are not edible by humans. Try arrowwood as a screen or tall hedge, in naturalistic bird and wildlife gardens, or toward the back of shrub borders.

Several fine cultivars are available, including compact Blue Muffin (5-7 ft. × 10-12 ft.), known for its abundant bright blue berries. For improved fruit production, plant dwarf Little Joe (3-4 ft. × 3-4 ft.) or Chicago Lustre (8-10 ft. × 8-10 ft.) nearby for cross-pollination. The adaptable cultivar 'Ralph Senior' (8-10 ft. × 10-12 ft.), also called Autumn Jazz, is especially valued for difficult sites like parking lot planting areas. A related species found in the wild in shaded woodland settings is spring-blooming maple-leaf viburnum (*V. acerifolium*; 3-6 ft. × 2-4 ft.),

SHRUBS

White flowers are just one of arrowwood's seasonal assets.

appreciated especially for its maple-shaped leaves that turn conspicuous purple-pink in fall. Its red fruits mature to purplish black.

CULTURE AND TIPS

Arrowwood generally requires little maintenance. It does best in sun or part sun, but tolerates shadier positions too. It thrives in average, slightly acid, well-drained soils, even where soil is mostly sand or damp clay. Seaside locations and those under black walnut trees are also tolerated. Prune old, dead, or dying stems in late winter for renewed growth in spring. To control size, tip prune just after bloom time and forfeit the berry crop for that year.

Few pests and diseases attack northern arrowwood except for invasive viburnum leaf beetle. This pest's larvae hatch in late spring and feed on the shrub's leaves for several weeks, causing severe damage. Adults lay eggs on young twigs, where they overwinter and hatch the following spring. Look for small, dark brown bumps along twigs from the current season between October and April—these are the beetles' eggs. Infested twigs should be removed and destroyed.

COMPANION PLANTS

When planting in a sunny location, partner northern arrowwood with beautyberry (*Callicarpa americana*) and shrubby St. John's wort

Arrowwood has attractive blue berries in summer that also make a nutritious meal for our native birds.

(*Hypericum prolificum*) for a pleasing combination of colors and textures. Effective perennial companions include orange coneflower (*Rudbeckia fulgida*), scarlet beebalm (*Monarda didyma*), and Maryland senna (*Senna marilandica*). Use native grasses like switchgrass (*Panicum virgatum*) for textural contrast, especially its cultivars 'Northwind', 'Shenandoah', and 'Cape Breeze'.

DID YOU KNOW?

Invaluable to wildlife, arrowwood provides food, cover, and nesting sites for many birds, particularly eastern bluebird, American robin, and gray catbird. It is a larval host plant for spring azure butterflies and hummingbird moths. When in flower, red admirals and eastern comma butterflies visit often for nectar, as do native bees and bumblebees. Interestingly, this plant's straight, sturdy yet pliable stems were prized by Native American hunters for use in making arrows, hence its common name.

Resources

RETAIL MAIL-ORDER RESOURCES FOR PLANTS

Bluestone Perennials: bluestoneperennials.com
Broken Arrow Nursery: brokenarrownursery.com
Digging Dog Nursery: diggingdog.com
Forest Farm: forestfarm.com
High Country Gardens: highcountrygardens.com
Izel Plants: izelplants.com
Mail Order Natives: mailordernatives.com
Nearly Native Nursery: nearlynativenursery.com
Plant Delights Nursery: plantdelights.com
Prairie Nursery: prairienursery.com
RareFind Nursery: rarefindnursery.com
Wood Thrush Natives: woodthrushnatives.com
Woodlanders: woodlanders.net

FURTHER READING

Armitage, Allan M. 2006. *Armitage's Native Plants for North American Gardens*. Portland, Oregon: Timber Press.

Clausen, Ruth Rogers. 2011. *50 Beautiful Deer-Resistant Plants*. Portland, Oregon: Timber Press.

Clausen, Ruth Rogers, and Thomas Christopher. 2015. *Essential Perennials*. Portland, Oregon: Timber Press.

Dirr, Michael A. 2011. *Dirr's Encyclopedia of Trees and Shrubs*. Portland, Oregon: Timber Press.

Dirr, Michael A., and Keith S. Warren. 2019. *The Tree Book*. Portland, Oregon: Timber Press.

Dove, Tony, and Ginger Woolridge. 2018. *Essential Native Trees and Shrubs for the Eastern United States*. Watertown, Massachusetts: Charlesbridge.

Gracie, Carol. 2012. *Spring Wildflowers of the Northeast*. Princeton, New Jersey: Princeton University Press.

Holm, Heather. 2014. *Pollinators of Native Plants: Attract, Observe and Identify Pollinators and Beneficial Insects with Native Plants.* Minnetonka, Minnesota: Pollination Press.

Leopold, Donald J. 2002. *Native Plants of the Northeast.* Portland, Oregon: Timber Press.

Mellinchamp, Larry. 2014. *Native Plants of the Southeast.* Portland, Oregon: Timber Press.

Monheim, Eva. 2020. *Shrubs & Hedges: Discover, Grow, and Care for the World's Most Popular Plants.* Beverly, Massachusetts: Cool Springs Press.

Rainer, Thomas, and Claudia West. 2015. *Planting in a Post-Wild World.* Portland, Oregon: Timber Press.

The Xerces Society. 2016. *100 Plants to Feed the Bees.* North Adams, Massachusetts: Storey Publishing.

USEFUL WEBSITES

Grow Native! Missouri Prairie Foundation: grownative.org/native-plant-info/ plant-picker/

Lady Bird Johnson Wildflower Center: wildflower.org

Missouri Botanical Garden: missouribotanicalgarden.org

Mt. Cuba Center: mtcubacenter.org

National Wildlife Federation: nwf.org

USDA Plant Hardiness Zone Map: planthardiness.ars.usda.gov

USDA Native Plants Database: plants.usda.gov

Photo Credits

Index

RANDY BACHAND

GREGORY D. TEPPER

RUTH ROGERS CLAUSEN is the author of *50 Beautiful Deer-Resistant Plants*, and co-author of *Essential Perennials* and *The Proven Winners Garden Book*. She received a Quill and Trowel award from the Garden Writers Association (now Garden Communicators International) and has written for the American Garden Guides series. She is the former horticulture editor for *Country Living Garden* magazine and a long-time contributor to *Country Gardens* magazine. Ruth lectures widely at horticultural conventions and symposia, flower shows, and to garden societies and clubs. In 2017, she was awarded the Garden Media Award by the Perennial Plant Association.

GREGORY D. TEPPER is a professional horticulturist, lecturer, consultant, and life-long native plant enthusiast. He is currently horticulturist at the Arboretum at Laurel Hill and West Laurel Hill Cemeteries in Philadelphia, Pennsylvania, and previously held the positions of director of horticulture at Mt. Cuba Center in Hockessin, Delaware, and director of horticulture and board member at Delaware Botanic Gardens, where he was instrumental in developing the garden's initial horticultural mission and implementing a two-acre meadow designed by world-renowned garden designer Piet Oudolf.